The apostles
of Jesus

© Day One Publications 2005
First printed 2005

ISBN 1-903087-94-5

9 781903 087947 >

Unless otherwise stated, all Scripture quotations are from the
New International Version copyright © 1973, 1978, 1984

British Library Cataloguing in Publication Data available

Published by Day One Publications
Ryelands Road, Leominster, HR6 8NZ
☎ 01568 613 740 FAX 01568 611 473
email—sales@dayone.co.uk
web site—www.dayone.co.uk
North American—e-mail—sales@dayonebookstore.com
North American—web site—www.dayonebookstore.com

Designed by Steve Devane and printed by Gutenberg Press, Malta

Contents

Introduction

John Wesley, the eighteenth century Methodist evangelist, regularly preached fifteen sermons a week. In the light of this, according to the busyness of Jesus recorded in the Gospels, it is unlikely that Jesus preached and taught publicly for less than twenty hours a week. If so, and if he spoke at one hundred and thirty words per minute, which is a normal lecture speed, then in one year of his public ministry our Lord would have delivered 8,112,000 words; and in three years that would amount to around twenty-four and a half million words. But only twenty-four thousand are recorded in the Bible, which means that we have merely one thousandth part of what Jesus taught during his public ministry. In bringing 'all things' to the memory of the disciples (John 14:26), the Holy Spirit must have been very selective. This is confirmed by John, who informs us that we have only a small part of the miracles, interviews and actions of Jesus (John 21:24–25).

It is perhaps hardly surprising, therefore, that for all their importance, most of the apostles have very little on record either of what they said or what they did. James the son of Alphaeus does not have a single word recorded and is mentioned only in the lists of the Twelve and as the son of Mary in Mark 15:40; we know even less about Simon the Zealot! Unless we identify Bartholomew with the Nathanael of John's Gospel, where he enjoyed a very brief interview with Jesus and went fishing with a few of the disciples after the crucifixion, we know nothing about him either. Similarly, there are no recorded words of Matthew, and it is only his dramatic call to discipleship and the meal that he put on afterwards for his cronies to meet Jesus, that draws our attention to him at all.

More surprising is the fact that even Andrew has less than thirty words credited to him, and John—surely one of the leading apostles—offers us not a single word of his own, apart from two or three phrases that he shares either with his brother James or with Peter. We know nothing about Thomas, apart from what John tells us in his Gospel, but then, John seemed to have a particular interest in some of these lesser known apostles. Even Judas the betrayer has more to say for himself than most of the apostles. So, whatever we read Jesus and his apostles said and did, and whoever we read they met, all this must be very significant because there was a vast amount more that could have been recorded.

For this reason, although they are all apostles who we imagine were some of the 'big' characters of the New Testament, considering how little we are told about most of them and what they all were before their call to follow Christ, they fit well into the pattern of God's little people. Apart from Peter and John, they all virtually pass from our view as individuals after the first chapter of Acts. James only reappears in time to be executed by Herod. Whilst there is inevitably plenty of legend to follow them all beyond the pages of Scripture, there is very little that we can be certain of—and that goes for Peter and John as well. Is this an accidental oversight of history, or the deliberate purpose of God? They, like all of us, had a relatively small window of opportunity to serve Christ before they were hurried into the eternal kingdom. Their legacy never had a name-tag attached for the following generations to read: the apostles started no movements under their own name and erected no buildings; even the claim that Peter was the founder of the church at Rome is of more than dubious reliability.

Under the covenant recorded in the Old Testament a male heir was crucial, and to be able to trace one's family roots was essential, but when the new and lasting covenant was ushered in with the advent of the Son of God, all this became irrelevant. Not one of the apostles left a blood line that we can trace, Peter is the only apostle of whom we have any detail about his domestic life, and even the theology of an unbroken apostolic succession is a wishful myth. When Paul heard a hint of apostolic parties, he rejected such ideas immediately (1 Corinthians 1:12–13). The only movement known to have adopted the name of an apostle, the Paulicians, was a heretical group who came to birth in Armenia in the mid-seventh century and struggled on for a long time before becoming extinct some twelve hundred years later.

Like all of us, these little people worshipped, worked and went. Admittedly books have been written on the life and letters of Peter, and the writings of John, but that is all. There is simply insufficient material for a single book on any of the others. Sadly, and perhaps significantly, we could write more about Judas Iscariot than Bartholomew, Matthew, James the son of Alphaeus, and Thaddaeus combined. Yet these are the 'apostles'— no less! But then, the whole purpose of our lives, as theirs, is not that we should leave a name for ourselves but that we should exalt the name of

Christ. John the Baptist set the compass bearing for the journey of the apostles of Christ—and for all who follow them—when he announced: 'He must become greater; I must become less' (John 3:30). Few have exhibited this so well as the twelve apostles.

It may help to avoid some confusion if we remember that Jesus himself had at least four brothers who are mentioned in the Gospels: James, Joseph, Simon and Judas (Matthew 13:55) and three of these share the same name as apostles. Each of them appears to have been persuaded of who Christ was only after the resurrection—which is remarkable since they grew up with their unusual brother—and later James became the leading elder in Jerusalem and the author of the New Testament letter; his brother Jude also left us a letter.

What is particularly interesting is the close relationship that many of the apostles shared. Peter and Andrew were brothers, as were James and John. Matthew and James were both sons of Alphaeus and this could mean they were brothers also, though we are not told so. More than this, if James and John were sons of Salome, then they were cousins of Jesus because Salome was very likely the sister of Mary. But there were close business ties also. Peter, Andrew, James and John worked together in a fishing syndicate, and almost certainly Philip and possibly Thomas were in the same trade; Bartholomew (Nathanael) was very likely a fisherman too, which means that seven of the twelve were fishermen. Of the rest, we know only the profession of Matthew and the political affiliation of Simon the Zealot; of the other three we can only guess.

Having said all this, if we believe that the Holy Spirit has carefully selected the information we are given, then it is not at all impossible to make some significant judgements about the character of each of the apostles, without resorting to wild speculation. As with the little people in the letters of Paul, I have not provided much application of the lessons learnt from these lives. My purpose has been to describe their characters with all the information we have available. The application speaks for itself.

Andrew—Simon Peter's brother

'The first thing Andrew did was to find his brother Simon and tell him, "We have found the Messiah"' John 1:41

If we make the reasonable assumption that the incidents recorded in John 1 reveal the earliest relationship of Jesus with his disciples, then Andrew is the first named disciple and the first to follow the Lord. And if we believe that the Gospels are not haphazard reports of the life and teaching of Christ, then there is significance even in the simple fact of Andrew being the first disciple we are introduced to. The clue to that significance is found in precisely the way that he is introduced.

Andrew came from the little fishing town on the north coast of Galilee called Bethsaida (John 1:44). The name unsurprisingly means 'house of fishing' and it was just five miles along the coast from Capernaum, which was the more important customs post and military base situated in a richly fertile region. Later, Andrew must have moved to Capernaum where we find him living in the family home of his brother Peter. Perhaps Andrew never married, or at least there is no mention of his own family.

We know nothing of his early life or how he became a disciple of John the Baptist. Clearly this can only be explained as the purpose of God, because there is little to mark him out as a revolutionary or zealous follower of a rugged and fiery prophet. He seems to have formed a close friendship with Philip, not only because Philip, when approached by the Greeks, immediately took them to Andrew (John 12:20–22), but both Mark and John place Philip immediately after Andrew in the list of the apostles, as if that was a very natural association. They are the only apostles with a Greek name, so this may have thrown them into each others company; his name means 'manly'. Philip also lived in Bethsaida and was very likely a fisherman, so they had much else in common.

To be a brother of the impetuous Peter, whose clear leadership qualities stand out in bold letters throughout the New Testament, could not have been easy! And all the evidence is that Andrew was a quiet, thoughtful man who was slow to act and speak, and was only too ready to slip into the background. He lived in the shadow of an energetic brother. Perhaps it was this quiet and retiring nature that so annoyed Peter, and he probably had Andrew firmly in mind when he asked Jesus: 'Lord, how many times shall I forgive my brother when he sins against me? Up to seven times?' (Matthew 18:21).

It is here in the beginning of the story of the call of the disciples that something of the character of Andrew is revealed. At the point where John introduces Andrew, his brother Peter had not come onto the scene, yet John refers to him as 'Andrew, Simon Peter's brother.' This is emphasised by John when there seems no need for such a designation 'Andrew, Simon Peter's brother' (John 6:8)—there is no other Andrew in the New Testament with whom he could possibly be mistaken. Even Matthew refers to 'Peter and his brother Andrew' (Matthew 10:2) and Mark refers to 'the home of Simon and Andrew' in that order (Mark 1:29). To many men that would be galling! To live in the shadow of a brother who is so well known, and to realise that you yourself can only be identified as his brother, would be hard for many to cope with; but I do not believe it posed any threat to Andrew—and that is precisely why the Holy Spirit has chosen to introduce him to us in this way.

Andrew seems to have become accustomed to play a subordinate role alongside his more extrovert and impetuous brother. There were three apostles taken into the inner circle of training by Jesus: Peter, James and John. The latter two were brothers and also part of the same fishing consortium with Peter and Andrew; so did Andrew never wonder why he was not included with his own brother in this exclusive group of associates? Significantly, Andrew's name appears just thirteen times in the Gospels and Acts, whilst that of Peter occurs more than one hundred and sixty times. However, the few references to Andrew are more than significant.

Andrew, the disciple of John the Baptist
We do not know for certain who the other disciple was who is referred to as the companion of Andrew on this momentous day when Andrew first met

Jesus (John 1:35–37). More than likely it was the apostle John himself. What is clear is that Andrew and his friend had heard John the Baptist directing their attention to Jesus as 'the Lamb of God, who takes away the sin of the world' (1:29) and they were so eager not to miss anything, that they were with John early the next day—and they appear to have been the only ones who were. This time they followed John's directions and met with Christ. Presumably Peter was busy with his fishing and his family, but Andrew took time out to learn more from the Baptist.

Andrew had clearly been listening intently to the teaching of this outspoken prophet, and what he heard was making a lot of sense. The fact that Andrew is described as a 'disciple' of John—something never claimed for Peter—indicates that he had already begun to pull away from his occupation as a fisherman and felt irresistibly drawn, not so much to the Baptist himself, but to the one about whom he was so passionately preaching. This is what Andrew heard from the uncompromising preacher:

'He who comes after me has surpassed me because he was before me' (John 1:15).

'I am not the Christ' (v 20).

'I am the voice of one calling in the desert, "Make straight the way for the Lord"' (v 23).

'Look, the Lamb of God who takes away the sin of the world' (v 29).

'He … will baptise with the Holy Spirit' (v 33).

'I have seen and I testify that this is the Son of God' (v 34).

Andrew did not understand it all: the Christ—the Lord—the Lamb of God—the Son of God—but he understood enough, and he was convinced that Jesus of Nazareth was the Messiah promised all through the Hebrew Scriptures; he was the ultimate and only sacrifice for sin whose unique relationship with God qualified him to forgive sin and baptise with the Holy Spirit. All this he had learnt from John the Baptist. Many of the disciples of John understood little more than his message of repentance from sin; but Andrew listened and learned—and when the moment of introduction came, he was ready to follow Christ. Perhaps this was annoying Peter: Andrew was spending so much time with this fiery prophet and so little time fishing; did he not realise there was a family to feed? For his part, Andrew maintained his priorities; he was looking for the Messiah and was coming to the conclusion that, at last, he had found him.

At 4 o'clock on that afternoon, John lost two of his most loyal and attentive disciples, and Jesus gained two of his. They never returned to the Baptist. But a Christian messenger is only successful when his hearers are attracted to Christ. That was a lesson Andrew learnt from his old mentor, and one that he never forgot. The signpost is not the destination. Some leaders are good at pointing people to Christianity, the Bible, or themselves, but they do not lead us to Christ.

Andrew as the brother of Peter

The first words to Jesus by Andrew and his friend bear all the marks of an embarrassed and blustering introduction! Whilst they followed Jesus (John 1:37), they were probably discussing how they should approach him and which one would do it, when suddenly Jesus turned round and caught them by surprise. 'What do you want?' was hardly the question they had been expecting and they were thrown off guard. They at least addressed him with respect: 'Rabbi', but beyond that one gets the impression that they did not know how to continue and so blurted out the first thing that came to mind: 'Where are you staying?' That was hardly a profound expression of all they had learnt from the Baptist, and it did not exactly reveal their growing awareness of the deep significance of this occasion. But his simple invitation to join him for the evening put them at ease, and a few short hours in company with the Son of God dispelled any remaining doubts they may have had. Andrew was convinced and, we may say, converted.

What happened next will always be to the credit of Andrew. With John he was the first to hear the Baptist point to Christ, and the first to become a disciple of the Messiah: but he was also the first disciple to introduce someone to the Saviour—his own brother. Andrew was the first home missionary. Later, when Jesus issued a more formal call to Andrew and Peter, he assured them that they would become 'fishers of men' (Matthew 4:19);

that was news to Peter, but his brother had already begun this new type of fishing.

It seems to have been a fairly packed home in Capernaum: Peter lived there with his wife and her mother, and perhaps his father-in-law as well, and Andrew made up the number. Inevitably they got on each other's nerves at times and this may be why, outside the home Andrew spent his time with Philip. Because of the opposite natures of Andrew and Peter, they probably sparked each other often.

But Andrew was a true brother: 'The first thing Andrew did was to find his brother Simon ...' (John 1:41–42). It is clear that this adverb describing his action is deliberate: this was the very first thing Andrew did. Nothing else mattered but that Peter should share the great news that the long expected Messiah was here and Peter must come and meet him for himself. Whatever their differences, Andrew had only the welfare of his brother at heart, and the very best thing he could do for him was to introduce him to the Messiah. This is precisely how most people are introduced to Christ, as all statistics on evangelism show, and it is why Jesus specifically told both · the paralysed man and the Gadarene demon-possessed to 'go home' immediately after their healing (Matthew 9:6; Mark 5:18).

Almost at once, Andrew began to take a second place to Peter. It is Peter who received the name change from Simon to Cephas (Peter), and from now on Andrew is significant chiefly as Peter's brother. But that would not have bothered Andrew at all. What Andrew could not have imagined, was the valuable legacy that he would leave to the church of the future by introducing his brother to Jesus. Whoever knows the ultimate importance of leading one person to Christ?

Andrew as the disciple of Christ

Andrew's official call to be a disciple, along with his brother, is recorded in Matthew 4:18 'As Jesus was walking beside the Sea of Galilee, he saw two brothers, Simon called Peter and his brother Andrew ... "Come, follow me" Jesus said, "and I will make you fishers of men"'. Their response was immediate and unconditional: 'At once they left their nets and followed him.' Later the Twelve received their commissioning as apostles and were sent out on a preaching and healing ministry, but once again, Andrew is second in line to his brother: 'These are the names of the twelve apostles: first, Simon (who is called Peter) and his brother Andrew ...' (Matthew 10:2). In Mark's list he is fourth after Peter, James and John (Mark 3:18).

However, whilst Andrew shared all this with his brother, there are three occasions, mentioned only in John's Gospel, when he appears in his own right, and they each reveal his practical faith. One of God's 'little people' he may be, but he was by no means insignificant in the work of the kingdom.

The first occasion is found when Jesus had been teaching a large crowd and they ran out of daylight, food and ideas. Jesus tested the disciples by posing a question to Philip: 'Where shall we buy bread for these people to eat?' (John 6:5). Philip had no idea and said so. If they had eight months wages it would not be enough to buy what is needed—besides, where would they find so much at this time of day?

Meanwhile Andrew, with a little more practical common sense and perhaps a little more faith than Philip, had been casting around to see what they could muster; a lad with five cakes of barley bread and two small fish was the best he could offer and that seemed to be derisory in view of the need: 'How far will they go among so many?' (John 6:9). But full marks to Andrew for trying. His faith may not have been great, but he would not give up. The very fact that he offered the meagre supplies to Jesus must say something about his emerging confidence in the Son of God. He need not have suggested the food at all; surely the other disciples would scoff at his stupidity. But with half a mind on the possibilities he took a chance. We can imagine this thoughtful disciple pondering: 'I wonder if ...' as he took the bread and fish to Jesus.

When, many years later, the apostle James wrote about prayer and faith, he made a highly significant association. *The English Standard Version* captures the meaning well: 'The prayer of a righteous person has great power as it is working' (James 5:16). We might paraphrase the Greek in this way: 'The prayer of a righteous man has great power when it goes into action.' The emphasis is upon faith in action. Too often we do not receive because we do not ask; but as we ask, even with small and diffident faith, our faith grows and even more so as the Lord responds. That was exactly the experience of Andrew here. Hesitatingly he offered a handful of bread and fish, but there must have been some confidence in his action or he would not have bothered to offer such a paltry amount in the first place. His confidence must have been in Christ, certainly not in his own faith or in the bread and fish. Here was a clear example of what Jesus would later teach about faith as small as a grain of mustard seed (Matthew 17:20); it was not how much faith that mattered, but where the faith was placed.

The second occasion when the faith of Andrew shone was when his friend Philip was approached by a group of Greeks with the request that they would like to meet with Jesus, if only for a brief interview. It was the final week in our Lord's life and, by design, this was the Passover week. Jerusalem was buzzing with excited activity, and not only Jews by birth, but many Jewish proselytes—those who had converted to Judaism—were in the city for the occasion. Philip was unsure how he should react to the request. Jesus had made it clear that his primary ministry was to ' the lost sheep of Israel' (Matthew 10:6) and the apostles themselves had never been sent beyond Israel. Besides, Jesus was very busy at this time, and these were only Greeks. So Philip went to discuss the matter with his friend Andrew.

For his part, Andrew had no such doubts. He had learnt enough about Jesus to know that, busy though he was, the Son of God would always have time for those who looked for him—his own experience had taught him that. He had learned from the miraculous feeding of the five thousand men, plus women and children, that it was always worth taking the problem to Jesus and allowing him to decide the outcome. But notice that Andrew did not rush to Jesus on his own: 'Andrew and Philip in turn told Jesus' (John 12:22). There is a simple humility in that phrase; Andrew was not looking for honour or gratitude from the Greeks for effecting the interview, instead he took Philip along with him.

Just as Andrew has the honour of being the first home missionary, so he has the honour of being the first foreign missionary also. Quietly and in an unassuming way, Andrew began the great commission that Christ had not yet given: to reach out to those who lay beyond the borders of Israel. It would have been all too easy for Andrew to have responded that they had been commanded to preach only to the 'lost sheep of Israel' and that Jesus was not really interested in those from regions beyond. But these 'foreigners' mattered to Andrew as they mattered to his Master—and just as much as Peter had mattered to him. He had become a home missionary even before Jesus assured him that he would be a fisher of men, and now he became an evangelist to those from overseas just before Jesus declared 'I ... will draw all men to myself' (John 12:32). In fact, it was Andrew's action that gave Jesus his cue to make his universal offer.

The third reference to Andrew in John's Gospel places him in company with the inner circle of disciples: Peter, James and John. Jesus had just made a mysterious prophecy about the destruction of the Temple, and when he was on his own 'Peter, James, John and Andrew asked him privately, "Tell us when will these things happen? And what will be the sign that they are all about to be fulfilled?"' (Mark 13:3–4). Andrew had been there right at the start when John the Baptist heralded the kingdom, and Andrew was anxious to be involved in all future developments. What followed was more than they could have expected—a long explanation of the signs of the end times. It would be typical of Andrew that his thoughtful and enquiring mind would want to be in on any question that would take him deeper into an explanation of the future of the kingdom.

The final mention of Andrew places him with the disciples in a prayer meeting (Acts 1:13–14). Once again he is fourth in the list after the inner circle. Perhaps the Holy Spirit wants us to notice that we first meet Andrew when he was eager to find Christ and bring his brother to the Saviour, and we take leave of him in a prayer meeting. Andrew does not appear by name in the story of the early church in Acts, but there is no doubt at all that he was busy for his Master.

Tradition fills the silence of biblical history as it does with all the apostles. The fourth century church historian, Eusebius, informs us that Andrew may have worked as a missionary in Scythia, north of the Black Sea—and as a result he became the patron saint of Russia. Another tradition suggests that he evangelised in Achaia, a region on the south coast of Greece—perhaps he never lost an interest in the Greeks—and that he was crucified there by being tied to a cross to prolong his agony. Nearly seven hundred years after his death, Andrew became the patron saint of Scotland when, supposedly, one of his arms was brought to the town that now bears his name on the east coast!

Andrew is not a startling character: there is no dash and activity like Peter, no strong determination and unpredictable character like James and

John, and no dramatic conversion like Matthew. He appears to be quiet, thoughtful, persistent and unassuming—but his work was vital. He brought his brother to Christ and little realised what far-reaching results that would have. In fact, he seems to have learnt from John the Baptist that the most important task in life is not to make a name for oneself, but to bring people to Christ: his brother, a little boy with some bread and fish, and a party of Greeks. There are no impressive exploits, no crowds following him, no miracles recorded and no great preaching. But through Peter, thousands heard of Christ and millions have read his letters, through the young boy thousands were fed from one of Christ's most outstanding miracles, and through the Greeks our Lord finally revealed his purpose to reveal himself to the whole world as its only light.

Never underestimate the value of the small actions of God's little people. Far reaching results come from seemingly small actions. A Moravian missionary led John Wesley to Christ, an unknown elderly preacher led the teenage Charles Haddon Spurgeon to salvation, and though few will know the name of Isaac Marsden, his preaching in Nottingham led young William Booth to realise his need of salvation.

Peter—the Rock

'You are Simon son of John. You will be called Cephas' John 1:42

O f all the apostles, it may seem hard to place Peter as one of God's little people. He was a prominent, larger-than-life character, full of self confidence and with an almost pugnacious disposition. A man of contradictions: he could be hasty and impetuous but also thoughtful and discerning; he was essentially resolute and loyal and yet fearful and apprehensive. Peter stood foremost among the apostles, offering the boldest protests of trustworthy allegiance, and yet was the one who, next only to the betrayer himself, failed most publicly when the hour of testing came. One of the first to declare his belief in the divine Sonship of Christ— he has been described as the Luther among the apostles—yet he could stall when persuasive false teachers compromised the gospel.

On the other hand, when he toppled, Peter was not a man to stay down, and however hard his fall he would always return to the work his Master had called him to. Peter habitually voiced the thoughts of all the disciples— speaking when others feared to whisper—but he was not only their spokesman, he was obviously the man with drive and leadership. When Jesus slipped out of the house early to pray alone, it was 'Simon and his companions' who went to look for him (Mark 1:36), and when the disciples were at last convinced that Jesus really had risen from the dead, it was Peter who incongruously declared, 'I'm going out to fish', and the others meekly responded, 'We'll go with you' (John 21:3). Above all, Peter clearly possessed a sharp and alert mind, even though, along with all the apostles, he was at first so dull to grasp spiritual truths (Matthew 15:16).

Whilst we have only glimpses of most of the apostles, and it is hard to define their characters from the little information we possess, this is not true of Simon Peter. He appears so often in the records—his name occurs almost one hundred and seventy times in the Gospels and Acts, compared with just thirteen for his brother—that it is not difficult to describe his personality and assess the kind of man he was. This is a mark of the authenticity of the Bible. Clearly Peter is one of the 'heroes' of Scripture, and yet we view him in all his miserable failures as well as his successes. That reveals the Bible as an authentic record in an age when negative revelations about favourites were simply lost to history.

Peter, like his brother Andrew who first led him to Christ, was a fisherman born in Bethsaida at the northern tip of the lake of Galilee (John 1:44) but now living and working in Capernaum, just a few miles along the coast. Peter is the only disciple of whom we learn anything about his domestic arrangements—beyond the fact that at least some of the others were also married (1 Corinthians 9:5)—and we know that his mother-in-law lived with Peter and his wife (Matthew 8:14). At some point Andrew seems to have moved into the home with them, and it is quite possible that it was in this house that Jesus stayed when he took up residence in Capernaum (Matthew 4:13). Many years later, when Peter set out on his missionary travels after the ascension of Christ, his wife accompanied him (1 Corinthians 9:5). Incidentally, this makes him a most unlikely candidate as the supposed founder of the celibate pontiffs of the Roman Catholic denomination!

Both Bethsaida and Capernaum, whilst strongly nationalistic, were heavily influenced by Greek language and culture, and Peter's brother even had a Greek name; in fact 'Simon' is the Greek form of the Aramaic 'Simeon'. However, their father, Jonah, was clearly a Jew (Matthew 16:17). The family were brought up to be faithful Jews committed to the careful observance of the laws and ceremonies of the faith of Israel (Acts 10:14), and years later this strong attachment to Jewish culture would cause Peter to hesitate when confronted by the false teaching of the so called 'Judaeizers' (Galatians 2:11–13). He would have been fluent in both Aramaic and Greek, and he spoke with a strong north country accent that easily identified him from the region of northern Galilee (Matthew 26:73; Mark 14:70). Peter had received an adequate education, and the family apparently used the *Septuagint*, which was the Greek translation of the Hebrew Scriptures; certainly this was the version Peter shows familiarity with in his letters.

It is generally agreed that the two letters that bear his name in the New Testament were written in the polished Greek of an educated man; this very fact has led some to question his authorship of them, arguing that it would not be possible for a Galilean fisherman who had no 'higher education' to write in such a good style and with such a command of the Greek language. However, the sneer of the Sanhedrin recorded in Acts 4:13 that Peter and John were 'unschooled' (agrammatos) was intended as a deliberate 'put-down' to mask the fact that the authorities were 'astonished' at their learning.

For our part, we need not be astonished. The ability of a sharp and alert mind to learn fast with the right incentives has been more than adequately demonstrated in history: John Bunyan was a village pot-mender who became one of England's most renowned authors, William Carey was a country cobbler before becoming Professor of Bengali at Fort William College in India and a Fellow of the Linnaean Society; and John Newton, with only two years of inferior education to his name and a common sailor at the age of eleven, taught himself Hebrew and Greek, and could later correspond with Dutch theologians in Latin.

Peter's birth name was Simeon, a constant favourite with the Jews in Greek-speaking areas and by far the most common name in first century Palestine and Galilee; in fact it remained popular among Jews right across the empire for the next two or three centuries. There are seven men with this name in the Gospels and another two in Acts, so we may not be surprised that he soon picked up the distinguishing nickname of Peter. Simeon literally means 'snub-nosed', but since most babies are, we must not read anything into this!

The new name given to him by the Lord was *Cephas* in the Aramaic, but it translated into *Petros* in the Greek (John 1:42). In reality *Petros* was not a proper name at all, and there is no evidence of its use among Jews at this time; among Jewish inscriptions the only appearance is in reference to a Jew who had become a Christian and had taken this as his 'Christian' name—and even that does not occur until the fifth century! However, during the early centuries of the church, after the resurrection and ascension of Christ, it gradually became a popular Christian name, and is found in the first century catacombs in Rome. So 'Peter' is a uniquely Christian name. The word meant 'a rock', and our Lord clearly had the significance of this in mind when he gave it to Peter.

However, 'Peter' was only a nickname, and when Matthew introduces him at first, he refers to him as 'Simon who is called Peter' (4:18), and similarly in his list of the apostles (10:2). At the confession of Peter at Caesarea Phillip he is 'Simon Peter' (16:16), and when our Lord addressed him, on each occasion it was the name 'Simon' that he used (16:17 and 17:25). For his part, Mark uses 'Simon' up until the call of the Twelve, and from there on it is 'Peter'; however, once again, the Lord addressed him in Gethsemane as 'Simon' (14:37). Luke follows a similar line, with the exception of 5:8 where 'Simon Peter' is used. John generally prefers 'Simon Peter' unless the Lord is addressing him. From all this, it is clear that Jesus was not so much presenting Simon with a new name—since he himself continued to use his birth name when speaking to him—but was establishing a new credential for him as one who would become a rock-like man. However, the word *Petros* increasingly slipped into more common use as his nickname which, after his martyrdom, became a respected name for boys born into a Christian home.

Peter's special relationship with Jesus, and his leadership among the apostles, is clear from the fact that his name always occurs first in the lists and that he was, according to Paul, the first apostle to see the risen Christ (1 Corinthians 15:5 and compare Luke 24:34)). The career of Peter falls naturally into the two divisions of an apostle before and after Pentecost, though for our purpose it is his character that we are interested in above all.

Peter, the positives of a born leader

When we look at the lives of James and John we will probe again at the reason why Jesus selected three men for his inner circle: Peter, James and John. It is sufficient here to state that Peter was a natural leader and this is evident by our Lord's command to him on the precise occasion when he warned the apostle of his saddest moment of failure: 'When you have turned back, strengthen your brothers' (Luke 22:32). Later, the women at the tomb were told by the angel specifically to share the news of the resurrection with the disciples *and Peter* (Mark 16:7). Peter was frequently the spokesman for the whole group and although he often spoke rashly, he was at least quick thinking and decisive. It was Peter who volunteered to get out of the boat on the lake (Matthew 14:29), who unhesitatingly drew his sword in Gethsemane (John 18:10), who ran straight into the tomb while John had hesitated outside (John 20:6), and who jumped overboard to reach the risen Christ first on the beach (John 21:7). Even the collectors of the temple-tax seem to have recognised Peter as the leader of the group when they approached him to enquire whether or not Jesus was prepared to pay this tax (Matthew 17:24).

From the evidence of the post-Pentecost church, it is clear that Peter was a significant figure in the emerging world mission led by the apostles, and our Lord was preparing him for this. The Master knew that Peter would one day write important letters to steady the nerves of young Christians across the empire at a time of growing persecution, and that his experience on the 'mount of transfiguration' would be a valuable asset at such a time (see 2 Peter 1:16–18). All this lay behind the simple command to 'take care of my sheep' (John 21:16).

Resolute loyalty

A mark of Peter's emerging leadership was paradoxically seen in his hasty and impetuous actions. Of the four bold acts mentioned above: on the lake, in the garden, at the tomb, and beside the shore, Peter must have immediately regretted the first two! In the same way, he would often speak first and allow cautious wisdom to catch up later. It was Peter who insisted to Jesus that arrest, suffering, death and resurrection in Jerusalem 'shall never happen to you' (Matthew 16:22), and who foolishly suggested that he, with James and John, should make three little tents on the mount of transfiguration for Jesus, Moses and Elijah (Matthew 17:4); it was Peter who blurted out the question about how often he should forgive Andrew in family fracas (Matthew 18:21), and who boasted that he and the others had 'left everything to follow you' and so what would there be in it for them? (Matthew 19:27). It was also Peter who, when Jesus spoke of leaving them, wanted at once to know where he was going (John 13:36), and who cursed and swore that he did not even know who Jesus was (Matthew 26:74), and who, when challenged yet again to follow Christ, immediately swung the spotlight on John with the enquiry: 'Lord, what about him?' (John 21:21). In reality, none of this marks heavily against him. Peter was in training, and these verbal blunders came from a man of decisive action and determined loyalty.

This resolute loyalty was all to his credit. He may have lacked courage at the critical hour, but he did not lack resolve. Right at the start, together with his brother Andrew, Peter left his fishing career to follow Christ (Mark 1:16–18). Later he assured Jesus that though all the other disciples would fall away on account of Christ: 'I never will ... Even if I have to die with you, I will never disown you... Lord, I am ready to go with you to prison and to death ... I will lay down my life for you' (Matthew 26:33–35, Luke 22:33 and John 13:37). Although he would fail at the first time of asking, there is no doubt that Peter sincerely meant what he promised, and years later he would fulfil that pledge to the very letter. Even before the arrest of Jesus, it was doubtless Peter who had made a quick inventory of the apostle's military hardware: 'See, Lord, here are two swords' (Luke 22:38), and he was not slow in using his when the moment came (John 18:10).

There is little doubt that when Jesus had forewarned that one of them would betray him, behind the whispered request to John: 'Ask him which one he means' (John 13:24), was an intention to settle the issue in his own way. It could only have been the restraining hand of God that stopped Peter from unsheathing his sword there and then on the betrayer. No leader can expect loyalty if he himself is not loyal. When the betrayer had left the room, almost immediately Peter was declaring, once more, his personal loyalty to Christ: 'Lord, why can't I follow you now? I will lay down my life for you' (John 13:37). He speaks only for himself here, wisely concluding that such a massive claim cannot be made on behalf of anyone but himself.

Peter may have fled with the others in the garden, but his courage returned just sufficiently for him to follow 'at a distance' (Matthew 26:58); once again, his intention was to remain loyal and to reverse his earlier cowardice. It is all too easy to criticise Peter for warming himself by the fire among the guards and servants in the palace courtyard (Luke 22:55), but at least he was there and, apart from John, none of the other apostles were even this close to the action. When recounting the whole miserable episode to John Mark years later, Peter did not spare himself, and painted a sad picture of words to his young scribe that must have broken his heart again at the memory of his wretched failure.

But even when he had so tragically, vehemently and even blasphemously denied his Master three times in the courtyard, the fact is that Peter made no excuses for himself and did not point to the disappearance of the other disciples in defence of his own failure. Instead, 'He went outside and wept bitterly' (Matthew 26:75). And 'bitterly' is not too strong to translate the word *pikros* in the Greek.

Sincere humility

There was a deep humility in Peter that must not be overlooked. Even before his call to be one of the apostles, Peter acknowledged the authority of Christ when he momentarily protested that a fruitless night's fishing was hardly likely to be redeemed by daylight, but then corrected himself with an obedient: 'But because you say so, I will let down the nets' (Luke 5:5). Here was an experienced fisherman giving way to the son of a village carpenter. In fact Peter's humility is seen in his response after the great catch of fish was landed: 'Go away from me, Lord; I am a sinful man!' (Luke 5:8). That was not mock meekness, Peter knew and felt all that he said.

In the same way, his protest at the last supper when Jesus washed his disciples feet: 'You shall never wash my feet' (John 13:8) was an objection based on a growing understanding of who Christ was and of his own unworthy status by contrast. Here was a man who undoubtedly loved Christ with a pure passion, and for all his weakness and failure, 'Peter was hurt because Jesus asked him the third time, "Do you love me?"' (John 21:17); it pained him that Jesus had to question his love. The word translated 'hurt' is used often in first century texts for an anxious care or grieving over the death of a loved one.

On more than one occasion Peter suffered the humiliation of being publicly rebuked by the Lord. In his poor attempt to walk on the water, he received no commendation from Jesus, only: 'You of little faith, why did you doubt?' (Matthew 14:31)—but at least he had accepted the challenge, which is more than can be said for the others. When he tried to dissuade Christ from heading out to Jerusalem and inevitable death, Peter was met with a response that must have cut through him like a knife: 'Get behind me, Satan! You are a stumbling-block to me; you do not have in mind the things of God, but the things of men' (Matthew 16:23); that harsh rebuke was intended to test the mettle he was made of: would he break under such a withering 'put-down'?

Similarly, when Jesus took Peter, James and John apart in Gethsemane to pray with him, it was Peter alone to whom the rebuke was aimed when they fell asleep on duty: 'Simon, are you asleep? Could you not keep watch for one hour?' (Mark 14:37), and when it happened a second time, even Peter was lost for words (v 40). Finally, when he defended the honour of Christ in Gethsemane, the only response from the Master was: 'Put your sword away' (John 18:11). Jesus was deliberately testing his humility, and not once did Peter try to defend his failures, or contrast himself with the rest of the group.

It may be significant that when all the apostles were gathered at the table for the last meal they enjoyed before Jesus' arrest, Peter appears to have taken the lowest place at the table. Since the couches around an Eastern table would be in the form of a horseshoe, the lowest part of the seating would be directly opposite the top; this would have placed Peter opposite John and explains why he could signal across the table to John who was on the right hand side of Jesus (John 13:23–24), and why Jesus could offer the bread first to Judas who was presumably on his left—all of this without the other apostles being aware of what was happening. In the light of the Lord's warning that he would deny him, Peter appears to have taken himself to the lowest part of the seating.

Peter's humility is seen also in the fact that when he provided information for Mark to compile his life of Christ, he did not omit the story of his tragic denial; though, interestingly, Mark's is the only Gospel not to mention the sword play in Gethsemane; was it that Peter later saw this as an evidence of his courage and loyalty and therefore hid anything that was to his personal credit? Painfully, he unfolded the story of his failure to Mark: '"I don't know or understand what you're talking about" … Again he denied it … He began to call down curses on himself and swore to them, "I don't know this man you're talking about"' (Mark 14:68–71). Earlier in the record, Peter had informed Mark of the warning of Christ: 'If anyone is ashamed of me and my words … the Son of Man will be ashamed of him when he comes in his Father's glory' (Mark 8:38). Only true repentance can wipe that stain away.

The fact that Peter 'broke down and wept bitterly' (Mark 14:72 and Matthew 26:75) when the horror of his denial shattered all his previous protests of selfless loyalty, speaks powerfully of a man who could feel the weight of his personal sin—and hated himself for it. A proud and conceited leader will never win true respect from those who follow him, but a leader who acknowledges and feels his own weakness will always stand higher in the estimation of others than in his own—and the strongest leader should know how to cry.

Thoughtful discernment

Peter's decisiveness, loyalty and humility as a leader was enhanced by his evidently thoughtful discernment. Early in the ministry of Jesus, the crowds following him began to swell to very pleasing proportions—at least as far as the apostles were concerned. However, at this point Jesus turned up the level of commitment that was expected of those who wished to be his disciples in such a way that it was calculated to discourage many. This certainly did not please the apostles, who complained: 'This is a hard teaching. Who can accept it?' (John 6:60). Their fears were soon justified because 'From this time many of his disciples turned back and no longer followed him' (v 66). At this point the Lord asked his twelve apostles: 'You do not want to leave too, do you?' (v 67).

Simon Peter's response was immediate and unhesitating: 'Lord, to whom shall we go? You have the words of eternal life. We believe and know that you are the Holy One of God' (v 68). Moments before, he had been 'grumbling' along with the others (v 61), but when the challenge came, Peter knew exactly where he stood. There was much he did not yet know or understand, but he had been long enough in the company of Christ to grasp that there was no other leader worth following, and he spoke decisively, and on the assumption that he spoke for them all: 'To whom shall *we* go... *We* believe.' This was no blind claim to loyalty; Peter stated his reasons why he had already come to this conclusion: he understood that Christ alone could offer eternal life, and that he was clearly the Messiah.

Some time later, Jesus was teaching about inner holiness, and in the course of his teaching, he used the picture that what comes out of a man's mouth makes him unclean, not what goes in (Matthew 15:10–11). Apparently the Pharisees understood what Jesus meant only too well, and they took exception to it; their minute insistence on food laws was far more important for them than inner holiness. For their part, the disciples did not understand it at all and Peter said so: 'Explain the parable to us' (v 15). Actually it was all fairly obvious and the Lord must have been exasperated at their stupidity—*and* he said so: 'Are you still so dull?' (v16). He then proceeded to spell out for them that the things that really makes a person morally and therefore spiritually unclean are not what they eat, but how they live, and such things as 'evil thoughts, theft, false testimony, and slander' come from a sinful heart. But the significance for us with regard to Peter is that, dull he may have been, but he did want to learn; it was Peter who asked the question.

On another occasion when Jesus had been teaching on the importance of being ready for the return of the Son of Man, he used the picture of servants at a wedding banquet. It was Peter who afterwards quizzed: 'Lord, are you telling this parable to us, or to everyone?' (Luke 12:41). The answer to that may be obvious to us, but it was clearly puzzling Peter and he wanted it clarified. It was also Peter who 'remembered' the events of the previous day and pointed out the withered fig tree, when perhaps the others had forgotten the incident (Mark 11:21).

This was all a prelude to Peter's great testimony of understanding at Caesarea Philippi. When Jesus asked the apostles what people were saying about him, they came up with answers; they had their ears to the ground and knew only too well what the popular conclusions were. But the real test lay in their Master's next question: 'But what about you? Who do you say I am?' (Matthew 16:15). Peter did not hesitate. Before anyone had time to draw breath, he was expressing his confident response: 'You are the Christ, the Son of the living God' (v 16). This was a small but significant advance on his previous claim. Peter was now certain that the Messiah was not simply a chosen prophet, but was the 'Son of the living God', and in the mind of any Jew, that was a claim to deity. Earlier, when Jesus claimed that God was his Father, many of the Jews tried all the harder to kill him 'because he was even calling God his own Father, making himself equal with God' (John 5:18).

But here at Caesarea Philippi, Peter even rose above the question of the Lord which was: 'Who do people say *the Son of Man* is?' (Matthew 16:13); that deliberately conditioned the response: 'Oh, we believe you *are* the Son of Man'. However, Peter rose higher than this when he affirmed Christ to be 'the Son of the living God.'

Throughout his time with Jesus, Peter was obviously watching and thinking. He was not simply enjoying the miracles, impressed by the teaching and marvelling at the character of his leader, he was putting it all together and thoughtfully working on the massive implications of it all: and Peter came to the conclusion that not only was Jesus the Messiah with a gospel that offered eternal life, but that he was God! The response of Jesus to Peter's claim revealed just how confident the Lord was that this apostle had proved himself fit for leadership: 'Blessed are you, Simon son of Jonah, for this was not revealed to you by man, but by my Father in heaven. And I tell you that you are Peter, and on this rock I will build my church, and the gates of Hades will not overcome it. I will give you the keys of the kingdom of heaven; whatever you bind on earth will be bound in heaven, and whatever you loose on earth will be loosed in heaven' (Matthew 16:17–19).

Centuries of debate, even conflict, have revolved around the identity of 'this rock'. One common interpretation is that Jesus spoke first to Peter 'you are Peter' (*petros* means 'rock') and then with some gesture pointed to himself and concluded 'on *this* rock (a slightly different word *petra*) I will build my church'. But there is no evidence of such a change in direction by the Lord, and we must beware of interpretations that demand invisible assumptions. The Roman Catholic interpretation is unequivocal: both references are to Peter who, together with his successors as bishops of Rome, are the rock on which the church is built. But why are two different words used to describe the rock if Jesus intended the same person? If he had meant the second word to refer to Peter also, it would have been more natural to say: 'You are Peter (*petros*) and upon *you* I will build my church'; then all doubt would have been removed. Whatever words Jesus used in his Aramaic, the Holy Spirit has given us two words in the Greek.

The most satisfactory conclusion is that the second word (*petra*) referred to the magnificent claim of Peter that Jesus was the Christ, the Son of the living God—on the truth of that, the church would be built in the future. This interpretation also has the advantage of being the oldest understanding of the passage—as far back as the church leader Origen early in the third century, when he had no historical debates to influence him. Significantly, three times in his later sermon on the day of Pentecost, Peter referred to Jesus of Nazareth as the Christ (Acts 2:31,36,38), and then twice in his sermon after the healing of the lame man (3:18,20), and on trial before the Sanhedrin, Peter was insistent that 'It is by the name of Jesus Christ of Nazareth' that the man had been healed (4:10). What is undeniable is that Peter himself, whether or not the *petra* referred to him, was eventually to be a firm encouragement to the other apostles and a leader in the church.

Peter, the practice of a trained leader

There are three incidents that marked out the Lord's special purpose for Peter. The first we have already seen at Caesarea Philippi, and there Jesus clearly gave Peter, together with the other apostles, the 'keys to the kingdom'—the commission to unlock the good news to the world. The second was the assurance given to this particular apostle that after all his protests of loyalty 'Satan has asked to sift you as wheat. But I have prayed for you, Simon, that your faith may not fail. And when you have turned back, strengthen your brothers' (Luke 22:31–32). From this feeble grain of wheat would come strength that would make the other apostles strong and firm. No one can be a strong spiritual leader until they have experienced the fires of testing and temptation and the deliverance that Christ offers. But the third occasion of the Lord's particular preparation for Peter was that painful interview with the risen Christ beside the lake.

It was appropriate that after Peter's threefold denial, his Lord should three times repeat the question: 'Simon, son of John, do you love me?' (John 21:15–17). This is the most reassuring episode in the whole story of Peter. The Bible is scattered with the stories of monumental failures, including Moses and David, yet in so many cases there is repentance, forgiveness and restoration to useful service. For all Peter's protests of loyalty, it is clear that the Lord was more interested in his love. It would be love for Christ that would motivate Peter in the future, not the bravado of unswerving courage. Above all, he wanted all his disciples to be men and women with a passionate love for the one who had died for them. For this reason, Christ repeated his question: 'Do you love me?', even to the point where Peter was hurt by the apparent distrust of his answers (v 17).

By the lake there had been an instant response when Jesus ordered Peter and his brother: 'Come, follow me' (Matthew 4:19–20); in the upper room Peter thought he was ready to follow Christ all the way: 'Lord, why can't I follow you now? I will lay down my life for you' (John 13:37); but the future would be far harder, and at the lakeside Jesus now wanted Peter to be sure of himself. Even then, he almost failed yet again. Turning to John, Peter wanted to know what the future of that disciple would be. But this was a secret with the Father and the Son. The true disciple should be concerned only to find his own place within the will of God and leave the Lord to take care of others; besides, it is the revealed will of God that we must obey, and not fret ourselves over the unknown things.

When the scene shifts from the Gospel records to the Acts of the Apostles, Peter was at once taking the lead. He is the one who stood up among the one hundred and twenty and reminded them all of the Scripture that demanded they should choose a successor to Judas the betrayer (Acts 1:15–22). Peter not only carefully quoted his Old Testament authority, but laid down the qualifications for the new apostle; and everyone agreed with him. The previous occasion his lead had been followed was when he despairingly declared 'I'm going out to fish' (John 21:3); now the fishing was going to be much bigger, and vastly more dangerous!

On the day of Pentecost, Peter was once again the clear leader, preaching the main sermon and defending the apostles against the charge of drunkenness. His sermon was full of Old Testament references and quotations. Similarly, when Peter and John were arrested after the healing of the lame man outside the temple—an incident where Peter took the lead—it was Peter who preached the sermon that led to their arrest and who was spokesman for their defence. His refusal to give way when threatened, and his insistence that they would go on preaching no matter what (Acts 4:8–12), shows Peter fulfilling his Master's command to 'strengthen your brothers' (Luke 22:32).

Having tasted the first experience of arrest among the Christians, Peter would also have to exercise the first discipline among the believers, and the tragic episode of Ananias and Sapphira (Acts 5:1–11) must have been a painful and fearful experience for him; he had surely not forgotten the time when he himself had lied passionately and repeatedly. Now his humility was being tested: with a power to discipline severely, and with miracles so remarkable and abundant that even his shadow could bring healing, resulting in huge crowds gathering, hundreds more 'added to their number', and everyone speaking well of them (5:12–16), it would be all too easy for Peter to take the praise for himself. But he had learned his lessons well, and the many bold claims followed by tragic failure recorded in the Gospels were constant reminders to Peter that he was fragile when sure of himself. Peter had learnt, long before Paul was even a Christian, that if anyone thinks he can stand firm, he had better be careful that he doesn't fall (1 Corinthians 10:12).

The first arrest, first discipline, and now the first imprisonment. Peter and John were singled out as the clear leaders of this new sect following their executed leader, Jesus of Nazareth, and they were thrown into prison. But another 'first'—angelic deliverance (Acts 5:19–20)—saw them once more on the streets proclaiming Christ, and this resulted in the first flogging for the sake of their Lord (v 40). When Peter was later thrown into prison by Herod, following the execution of the apostle James, he must have assumed that the promise of the Lord that his would be a martyr's death (John 21:19) was arriving sooner rather than later.

Before this, however, when the apostles heard that God had used the evangelism of Philip in a remarkable way among the Samaritans, it was only natural that they should suggest that Peter, along with John, should go to check out the work there. Peter's first clash was with a magician who had made a profession of faith—and Philip had even baptised him—but whose only connection with the truth was sharing the same birth name as Peter. The apostle's strength and courage as a leader was revealed when he opposed Simon the sorcerer and warned him of the grave consequences of persisting in his unbelief (Acts 8:18–24).

Peter enjoyed a fruitful period of evangelism in the region of Lydda, a city soon to be burnt by Nero, and Joppa, where he stayed with his namesake who was a leather worker (Acts 9:32–43). If the apostles collectively sent Peter to Samaria, it was the Lord alone who sent him from Joppa to Caesarea to lead Cornelius and his family to salvation. Surprisingly, Peter needed to learn a lesson about the willingness of God to save non-Jews, even though he had already seen a powerful spiritual work among the Samaritans. However, it was this involvement with Cornelius—a Roman centurion from Italy itself—that created the first significant division among the Christian community. A party of converted Jews insisted on Gentile converts adhering to many of the Jewish regulations, especially that of circumcision. This resulted in Peter defending his action clearly, boldly and successfully when he returned to Jerusalem (Acts 11:1–18). But that was not the end of the story.

Although the imprisonment and angelic deliverance of Peter recorded in Acts 12 is almost the last that we read of him in the Acts of the Apostles, it is by no means the end of his work. With the phrase that Peter 'left for another place' (Acts 12:17), he passes from the scene until the conference in Jerusalem (Acts 15:7–11); now Saul of Tarsus, renamed Paul, takes centre stage in the narrative, though James the brother of Jesus appears to become leader in Jerusalem. As to where Peter went, and what his ministry was, we have no information. We do know that Paul spent a fortnight with Peter when Paul first came up to Jerusalem with the specific objective of getting 'acquainted with him' (Galatians 1:18). On that occasion the rest of the Twelve appear to have been out of town since Paul confirms that he met only Peter among the apostles. It was fourteen years before Paul returned to the city (Galatians 2:1).

A moment of hesitation

However, the next time we hear of Peter, the news is not encouraging. Those Jewish converts who insisted upon the observance of Old Testament ceremonies did not leave the scene when Peter stood his ground after the Cornelius affair. They soon clashed with Paul—who was an even more powerful opponent—and it led eventually to the apostles calling all the leaders together in Jerusalem to thrash out the matter once for all. The account of this conference and its conclusion is recorded for us in Acts 15. However, before this, it is evident that Peter had taken his ministry primarily to the Jews and had been targeted by the 'Judaeizers'; under their influence he began to waver. Sadly, having once enjoyed fellowship with the Gentile converts, Peter was now withdrawing.

Paul is the one to reveal this to us in a sad comment in his letter to the Galatians, which was possibly written just before the conference in

Jerusalem. It is so significant that we should hear part of the story in Paul's own words:

'When Peter came to Antioch, I opposed him to his face, because he was clearly in the wrong. Before certain men came from James, he used to eat with the Gentiles. But when they arrived, he began to draw back and separate himself from the Gentiles because he was afraid of those who belonged to the circumcision group. The other Jews joined him in his hypocrisy, so that by their hypocrisy even Barnabas was led astray. When I saw that they were not acting in line with the truth of the gospel, I said to Peter in front of them all, "You are a Jew, yet you live like a Gentile and not like a Jew. How is it, then, that you force Gentiles to follow Jewish customs?"' (Galatians 2:11–14).

The old weakness of Peter was beginning to show: 'he was afraid'. For a brief interlude, Peter was back-tracking on a free offer of a free gospel; grace was clouded by law, and, as Paul pointed out, he who had abandoned so many of the Jewish customs as a disciple of Christ, was now insisting that those who had never been shackled in this way should fall into the snare of Jewish legality. Paul trounced him and clearly shamed him. The outcome was, fortunately for the sake of the gospel, positive; the conference in Jerusalem reasserted a gospel of free grace unfettered by Jewish ceremony, and in the discussions, Peter took a leading role on the side of truth (Acts 15:7–11). This, incidentally, is the last mention of Peter in the Acts of the Apostles. But the breach, though brief, had been serious, and he who had been commanded to strengthen his brothers, faltered and failed at a crucial moment, even dragging Barnabas, the son of encouragement, with him.

Back on track

Unfortunately the Corinthian church, ready to quarrel and divide over anything, had partisan groups, some of whom openly preferred the ministry of Peter, whilst others preferred the ministry of Apollos and a third group sided with Paul (1 Corinthians 1:11–12). There is no evidence that Peter himself was party to this, any more than Apollos was, and no doubt he applauded Paul's strident handling of the silly confusion. The worn out theory of some critics that Paul and Peter held opposing theology, has no evidence to support it either inside or outside the Bible. On the contrary, Peter wrote warmly of 'our dear brother Paul' and commended his wise letters to his own readers (2 Peter 3:15–16).

But if Peter teaches us anything, his is a life illustrating the restoration to valuable service of a Christian who falls, not once, but often, because the story of Peter's value to the Christian church in his day and beyond is not finished. Where Peter spent most of his remaining years is not known; it is even uncertain whether he ever arrived in Rome and almost certain that he was not responsible for the founding of the church there. But there are two letters that bear his name in the New Testament. There has never been any serious doubt that the first came from the apostle himself, and although there was some doubt about the second letter in the early centuries of the church, we need not delay on that issue now; it bears all the marks of Peter's writing.

Peter wrote to Christians scattered across the Empire who would shortly experience a time of severe persecution that would test the mettle of their faith (1 Peter 1:1–7); he who was so challenged about his own love for Christ reminded his readers that they had not enjoyed the privilege of seeing Christ, and yet still they love him (v 8). At the time of writing, Peter had put aside all his uncertainty about the gospel and was clear that redemption is through Christ alone and has nothing to do with the 'empty ways of life' whether of Jew or Gentile (vs 17–18). His letter encouraged the readers to realise who they are as the children of God, and to live in harmony to gain a good reputation in society. To this end Peter covered relationships in the nation, in the workplace, in the home and in the church. The primary thrust of his first letter was that the believers should live such quality lives that though men may hate their message, they would be forced to admire their morality. If the believers are to suffer at all, as they will, it must be for their Christian profession and not their bad lifestyle.

The second letter from Peter relied heavily upon his own experience of the transfigured Christ (Mark 9:2–13) encouraging his readers that he was an eyewitness of the majesty of Christ. In writing this, Peter must have smiled at himself as he recalled that on that occasion he came down from the mountain discussing with James and John what 'rising from the dead' meant (v 10). Those days of his blind ignorance and simple stupidity must have seemed a world away as he encouraged the scattered believers that they could implicitly trust the words of Scripture (2 Peter 1:16–21).

With the painful memories of his own close brush with heresy, Peter spent a deal of this letter (all of chapter two) warning against false teachers who 'introduce destructive heresies' (2:1). But apart from the Judaeizers, there were those who scoffed at the idea of Christ's return in glory; something that had mystified Peter a few years ago, but now thrilled him. He devoted all his closing remarks (almost the whole of chapter three) encouraging them to look forward with confidence to the coming of the Saviour to recreate the heavens and the earth.

With the 'disappearance' of Peter from the narrative in Acts after the conference in Jerusalem, it is hardly surprising that beyond the record of Scripture there has been no lack of legends to fill in the gaps. The most well-known comes to us from the third century. Peter, having worked for twelve years among the Jews, arrived in Rome after Paul had, supposedly, left for Spain; Peter defeated the heretic, Simon Magus, in spiritual combat and having upset the emperor Nero, fled the city only to meet with Jesus on the road. When Peter asked his Lord where he was going (*Domine, quo vadis?*), Jesus replied that he was on his way to Rome to be crucified. At this, Peter returned to the city and was put to death by Nero, requesting only that he be crucified head down, being unworthy to copy his Master's death. In fact, there is no certainty that Peter was ever in Rome, though it was likely. There are also a number of writings that claim to come from the hand of Peter— the *Apocalypse of Peter*, the *Preachings of Peter*, and the *Acts of Peter*—but they all originated at some time during the second century, and most are fragmentary and often obscure.

Finally, there is a strong tradition, that carries far more weight than the above, that the Gospel of Mark was written under the direction of Peter. John Mark was the first term failure who so upset Paul that it caused a severe rift between Paul and Barnabas and yet who ended up as a close companion of Paul; this was something Peter could easily identify with! Papias, a Christian leader writing around the year AD 140, has left on record that: 'Mark, who was the interpreter of Peter, wrote down accurately all that he remembered, whether sayings or doings, of Christ; but not in order, for he was neither a hearer nor companion of the Lord.

Mark made no mistakes when he wrote down thus all things as he remembered them, for he concentrated on this alone not to omit anything that he had heard nor to include any false statement among them.' Given that John Mark was a young man in the time of Acts, he may well, in his old age, have been acquainted with Papias, and there is no reason to doubt the word of this early church leader. Peter, then, relayed all that was of special significance to him in the life and ministry of Christ, to this younger disciple who 'made no mistakes' when he wrote it all down. This also, was Peter's lasting legacy to the church.

Peter had been commissioned by his Master to feed and tend the flock. In spite of all his failure and weakness—or because of them—he carried that through to the end and ultimately gave his life for the Man he loved so strongly—exactly as Christ said he would.

Philip—faith without confidence

'Philip said, "Lord, show us the Father and that will be enough for us"' John 14:8

O ne of the most encouraging facts about the Bible is that everything in it matters. By that I mean there is significance in all parts of the Bible and nothing can be considered unnecessary or superfluous. This is not only true of its great theological statements, but of every statement. We cannot believe that 'all Scripture is God-breathed' (2 Timothy 3:16) and then relegate some parts to irrelevant obscurity. The doctrine of the significance of all Scripture is well illustrated in the story of God's little people. We do not learn much about them, and for the most part they flit only briefly across the pages of the Bible, but what we do learn is significant, and we are expected to ask the pertinent question: Why are we told what we are told—no more and no less? The information is not random or careless because the Holy Spirit is too precise to be wasteful of words.

There are four men with the name Philip in the New Testament, so perhaps we should dispose of three of them first. One Philip was a half-brother of Herod Antipas the tetrarch; he lived as a private citizen and his wife, Herodias, deserted him in favour of his half-brother who was denounced by John the Baptist for this act of adultery. Both were sons of Herod the Great (Matthew 14:3–4). Another son of Herod the Great carried the same name and is referred to in Luke 3:1 as 'Philip tetrarch of Iturea and Traconitis' over which he ruled for thirty-seven years; he was responsible for the construction of the city of Caesarea Philippi, which was partly named after him. He married the infamous Salome, daughter of Herodias (Matthew 14:1–12).

A third Philip, and very different from the previous two, was one of the seven men chosen to serve the early Christian community and who later became an evangelist; he was married with four daughters and settled, coincidentally, at Caesarea Philippi (Acts 6,8,21). After Acts 1:13 all references are to the evangelist and not the apostle. That this Philip is not to be confused with the apostle is clear from the fact that he was one of the seven elected to serve (Acts 6:5 and 21:8), and that when all the Christians were 'scattered throughout Judea and Samaria' except the apostles (8:1), Philip was one of those who had been 'scattered' (vs 4–5).

Our Philip, one of the first of the twelve apostles chosen by Christ, lived at Bethsaida, the home town of Andrew and Peter. He was most likely a fisherman also and struck up a special friendship with Andrew. James and John, together with their father Zebedee, also came from this little fishing community on the shores of Galilee, so Philip may have been part of the informal working syndicate.

Apart from his name in the lists of apostles, there are only four occasions when Philip is the centre of activity or conversation, and they are all in John's Gospel. It is probably a reflection of his own unassuming character that John held a particular interest for God's little people. On each occasion, Philip reveals something valuable about himself, and on each occasion he learns something of value about his Saviour.

His name is Greek and literally means 'lover of horses'—but it would be foolish to deduce more from this than that his parents liked the name, though the Greek connection could account for the group of Greeks approaching Philip to gain an interview with Jesus. He and Andrew were the only two among the apostles whose names were Greek rather than Jewish.

Philip recognised the Messiah

Although Philip is consistently placed fifth in the list of apostles, he was, in fact, the fourth disciple to be called by Jesus after Andrew and John and then Peter (John 1:43–48). Either through the influence of his friend, Andrew, or else through his own understanding, Philip immediately came to the conclusion that the man who called him from his fishing occupation was none other than the prophet of whom Moses spoke fifteen hundred years earlier (Deuteronomy 18:15). This was no small assumption because the Jews had long equated the prophet promised by Moses with their hoped-for Messiah. How did Philip come to this conclusion?

Since they were all fishermen together, it is likely that Andrew and Peter had spoken excitedly about their conversations with Jesus, and Andrew was in no doubt that this Jesus was the Messiah (John 1:41). However, what clearly settled it in Philip's mind was his own meeting with Jesus of Nazareth dismissed simply by John in a major understatement: 'Finding Philip, he said to him, "follow me"' (John 1:43).

We must appreciate the massive mind shift that took place in order that four very ordinary Galilean fishermen—Andrew, John, Peter and now Philip—became so totally convinced that this 'ordinary' Jew, identified by an extraordinary preacher, John the Baptist, was in fact the Messiah promised a millennium and a half earlier—and that he wanted *them* to be his disciples. With the passing centuries we have given these apostles of Jesus a status of special honour, but in their own day nobody did; in fact they were all, without exception, very little people. Their 'surprise' must have been every bit as great as that of Mary herself when the angel told her she would be the mother of God's Son, and of the shepherds when they realised that they were the first to see him.

Who did these fishermen think they were? But that, of course, is part of the plan of God. They were some of the most unlikely and unexpecting of men. Many years later Paul wrote: 'Brothers, think of what you were when you were called. Not many of you were wise by human standards; not many were influential; not many were of noble birth. But God chose the foolish things of the world to shame the wise; God chose the weak things of the world to shame the strong. He chose the lowly things of this world and the despised things—and the things that are not—to nullify the things that are, so that no-one may boast before him' (1 Corinthians 1:26–29).

The way Philip recommended the Messiah to Nathanael (John 1:45) is more than odd; it might even be considered the best way to prove that he was not the Messiah after all. In the first place, the phrase 'Jesus of Nazareth' introduced a place of origin that was nowhere linked with the Messiah in the Hebrew Scriptures or in any of the Rabbinical expectations of the coming Messiah. At the best reckoning, Nazareth was an out of the way, obscure and aloof frontier town, twenty miles distant from

Capernaum and with no connection to the spiritual well-being of Israel. And secondly, 'the son of Joseph' was pretty meaningless apart from reassuring Nathanael that Jesus had a known genealogy—for one generation at least! Philip could not even rise to the personal experience of the Samaritan woman who at least claimed, 'Come, see a man who told me everything I ever did. Could this be the Christ?' (John 4:29).

So what convinced them to follow Jesus so confidently? There had been no miracles, and no mention of the angels or the shepherds, the wise men or the supernatural star. That all happened a long way down south and many years back. There is nothing in the story so far to convince anyone that this man really is the Messiah. And that is surely deliberate. In each case the disciple met with Jesus. That may seem obvious to the point of being trite, but it is an essential fact. John the Baptist pointed out Jesus to Andrew and his friend, and they approached him themselves; then Andrew 'brought Simon to Jesus' and Jesus 'found' Philip; then Philip urged Nathanael to 'come and see'. The testimony of another can take a potential disciple of Christ only so far, beyond that, belief will only become a reality when Jesus of Nazareth is personally encountered. Not one of the disciples persuaded another: they reasoned and invited, but it was the encounter with Jesus himself that transformed them into disciples.

This Man radiated deity to those who had eyes to see. But that is always true for those who are 'called according to his purpose'. It is an irresistible call. And that was something else that Philip was to learn, but this time from Nathanael's encounter. Nathanael's sceptical response threw Philip off guard, and his only reply—and a wise one—was to invite him to meet Jesus for himself: 'Come and see'. In response to Nathanael's incredulous: 'How do you know me?', Jesus replied, 'I saw you while you were still under the fig-tree before Philip called you.' In the whole story to this point, this is the first indication of anything miraculous about Christ; whatever the 'fig-tree' incident referred to, clearly it registered with Nathanael that neither Philip nor anyone else could have known about that private moment when no one else was around. Philip was now learning that whilst he thought he was effecting an introduction between Jesus and Nathanael, in reality Jesus had the whole encounter planned long before; how long before, Philip could not possibly appreciate just yet.

Why did Jesus decide 'to leave for Galilee' (John 4:43). Clearly his intention was to call Philip and Nathanael. Philip also learned a vital lesson about the absolute knowledge of Jesus—a lesson that the apostles would re-learn on more than one occasion (John 2:22–24) and even to their own embarrassment (Mark 9:33–37). Significantly John records that Jesus found Philip, whilst Philip encouraged Nathanael 'we have found' Jesus (vs 43–45). Was Philip right? Well, yes and no. That was certainly how Philip saw the matter, but he had yet to learn that in reality he had been found. Scientists may or may not be correct when they suggest that some people in society have genes that predispose them to religion, but the fact is that in Christianity it is God finding the individual that makes all the difference.

If the purpose of John in writing his gospel was to display the power and majesty of Christ, then this was his secret weapon: the greatest evidence of Christ's sovereign authority was his power to change men and women, simply because of who he was rather than what he did—it still is. Millions read the stories of the miracles of Jesus, and remain unmoved and unsaved. But those who meet with Christ by faith, have a wholly different relationship with him. As a young upwardly mobile lawyer, Paul once knew about Christ—what he taught and did—and he hated him for it; he viewed him merely 'from a worldly point of view' but after he met with Christ personally he declared that he regarded Christ in this way no longer (2 Corinthians 5:16–17).

Philip betrayed his lack of faith

We next meet up with Philip when Jesus was more than half way through his three years of ministry (John 6:1–13). A great crowd had been hanging on the words of the Master for the best part of the day and now there *were* miracles and teaching—and a lot of both. We might conclude that Philip happened to be the unfortunate disciple passing by when Jesus threw out a test question: 'Where shall we buy bread for these people to eat?', but there were no mere 'happenings' in the ministry of Jesus. We are encouraged to cast our minds back to the Philip who responded so immediately to the call of Christ at the beginning, and then contrast it with his response now. Our Lord set a trap for Philip: his question was not 'What shall we do?' which might have led Philip to respond honestly 'I don't know. What can *you* do?'

but 'Where shall we buy bread?', which led the apostle to work out the impossibility of that route.

There had been much instruction and now was the time for examination. Jesus not only teaches, he tests. We read and see so much about Christ and his ways but we are so slow to learn. The events of our lives are intended to be associated with what we have learnt; we are supposed to listen and learn so that when circumstances come that we had not anticipated—whether for good or seemingly bad,—we know how to respond. Sometimes the Lord throws across our path a situation that appears to be providential, but in reality it is a test of our wisdom and our sensitivity to his teaching. 'Providential' events are not always the right way. This was the moment of Philip's test; surely he had seen and heard sufficient to convince him that Christ could master this situation.

Philip betrayed his lack of confidence supremely by his reply. A quick reckoning told him that the number of people present would need more than eight months wages to buy enough food for just a morsel each--even assuming there was anywhere up here in the hills where that amount of bread could be purchased. His reply in John 6:7 almost has a hint of sarcasm about it. Philip had less confidence in the Lord than the distraught father would have a little later when he recounted the sorry story of his son's illness to Jesus and added, 'But if you can do anything, take pity on us and help us' (Mark 9:22); at least he had some hope. The leper recorded in Mark 1:40 was well ahead of both Philip and the boy's father when he affirmed, 'If you are willing, you can make me clean.' He threw himself, not on the hope of Christ's ability, but on his willingness.

When Philip stammered his hopeless lack of faith, Andrew was at least taking some steps to fill the gap (John 6:8–9). We may be surprised at Philip's lack of faith in the ability of Christ, especially in the light of the fact that he himself had come to faith so quickly, and he had believed Christ was the Messiah with no more evidence than the testimony of the Hebrew Scriptures behind him and the face of the Son of God in front of him. Now he failed at the first serious challenge to his faith. Perhaps, though he was not unlike all of us in this: a giant leap of faith for one action one day is no guarantee that we will be kept from despair a day later. The lesson Philip would learn this time was the absolute authority of Christ. If he learnt about omniscience with Nathanael, he was learning about omnipotence with Andrew.

Philip was uncertain about a universal gospel

A group visiting Jerusalem from Greece for the Passover had heard of Jesus of Nazareth and, being proselytes to the faith of Israel with a deep interest in all things truly spiritual, they wanted to check out this man and his teaching. Doubtless they had been listening and watching, but they knew what Philip had already learned and now seemed to have forgotten: if they are to grasp the message fully, they must meet with Jesus personally (John 12:20–33).

They approached Philip not because he 'was from Bethsaida in Galilee' (John 12:21) but because his was one of only two of the apostles with a Greek name. Their request was simple: 'Sir, we would like to see Jesus.' Why was Philip's first reaction to go and tell Andrew? It cannot be because he was afraid to bother Jesus, or that he did not have access to the Master; there can be only one reason: he was not certain that this was a proper request. In other words, Philip was not yet convinced that Jesus had come for the whole world. Perhaps he had at least two occasions fixed in his mind: the first was when Jesus sent out the disciples on their healing and preaching tour and told them to go only to 'the lost sheep of Israel' (Matthew 10:6), and the second was when, in response to the Gentile woman from the region of Tyre and Sidon, he declared: 'I was sent only to the lost sheep of Israel' (Matthew 15:24). But Philip should have learnt by now that the first was only a temporary injunction, and the second was no more than a test of the woman's faith and sincerity; his subsequent action in healing the woman's child should have taught all the apostles a strong lesson.

Philip was quick to tell Nathanael, but very slow to introduce the Greeks to Jesus; for him, Christianity was still locked into Israel. But he should have known that the Messiah had a far bigger mission than only to Israel. John the Baptist announced Jesus as 'The Lamb of God who takes away the sin of the world' (John 1:29), Jesus himself had been more than ready to share the good news with a Samaritan woman and this had led to many of the Samaritans believing (4:29), he had declared himself to be 'the bread of

God who gives life to the world' (6:33,51), twice at least he had claimed to be 'the light of the world' (John 8:12; 9:5), and he promised that his message was for the world (8:26).

Soon, Philip and the others would be left in no doubt that they were to take the message 'to the ends of the earth' (Acts 1:8) and 'make disciples of all nations' (Matthew 28:19). But right now Jesus gave a more indirect jog towards world vision: 'When I am lifted up from the earth, I will draw all men to myself' (John 12:32). The fact that the church should be constantly engaged in world mission is one lesson of which the church in every age needs to be constantly reminded; we forget too soon and neglect this vital task.

Philip wanted to see the Father

It was shortly before the end. Gently the Master had been preparing his disciples to live without him; so many promises had been, and will be, poured into their minds in order to stiffen their resolve to stand alone. However, when he finally told them that he was about to leave, but not to worry because it was all part of a far greater plan, and, besides, he will return one day to take them to their prepared home with him—they were shattered and confused. They were like men groping blindly in the dark when all the time the light was shining brightly (John 14:1–14).

Thomas wanted to know exactly where Jesus was going because without that knowledge how could they be expected to follow him—entirely missing the point that Jesus had not told them to follow him but had promised he would return in person to collect them! For his part Philip wanted to see God the Father so that they would know what he was really like (v 8)—entirely missing what Christ had just said to them all: 'I am the way and the truth and the life. No-one comes to the Father except through me. If you really knew me, you would know my Father as well. From now on, you do know him and have seen him' (John 14:6).

Of all the lessons that Philip should have learnt by now, this was clearly the most important. Perhaps there is a note of exasperation in the voice of Jesus when he virtually repeated what he had just said: 'Don't you know me, Philip, even after I have been among you such a long time? Anyone who has seen me has seen the Father. How can you say, "Show us the Father"?

Don't you believe that I am in the Father, and that the Father is in me?' (vs 9–10). Three years, and all the miracles, the teaching, the quality of his life, and still they have not grasped the fundamental truth that Christ is God and perfectly reflects his Father. They had been three years with the one who was 'The radiance of God's glory and the exact representation of his being' (Hebrews 1:3)! To have seen Christ is to see God, and to know Christ is to know God. That is where it all began in the experience of Philip: he had met with Christ long before the miracles, or the teaching, or three years living alongside a man wholly without sin, and he believed! Yet now he faltered.

There is a despairing appeal by Christ in the words that follow: 'So long, Philip, and yet'. They were addressed primarily to Philip, though clearly all the disciples needed to hear. So long, so much and yet so little understanding. A plea for the spectacular, an appearing of God the Father, a theophany, a voice, a vision—something to convince them. There is nothing new in all this, it has been the error of the church for centuries, from the earliest times, through the Middle Ages, to the present day. But Philip would be offered nothing more than the church will ever be offered: the life and ministry of the one who 'is the radiance of God's glory and the exact representation of his being' (Hebrews 1:3). Philip had come full circle: he began with a view of Christ that fully persuaded him—and that is where he would finish also. There was nothing better on offer because there was nothing better that could be offered.

But many listen to the message about Jesus of Nazareth, with no more positive response than Philip. Surrounded by those who take his life and death and resurrection seriously, the Master laments, 'Don't you know me... even after I have been among you such a long time?' And, apart from the prayer meeting in Jerusalem, on that sad note, the Gospel record falls silent over the name of Philip.

Tradition, as ever, fills a few gaps. The apocryphal *Journeyings of Philip the Apostle* from the third century, sends him through Asia, where he finally settled in Hierapolis (in what is now Turkey), about 6 miles north of Laodicea. Here, according to the *Journeyings*, he was cruelly martyred being hung by the heels and accompanied by strange appearances. An inscription has been found dedicating the church in Hierapolis to 'the holy and glorious apostle and theologian Philip.' However, there is debate as to whether the Philip at Hierapolis was confused for Philip the evangelist, and so we are wiser to stay with all that we certainly know from the Scriptures, and no more.

Philip is revealed to us in the record of John's Gospel in all his weakness—'faith without confidence' as one commentator has described it. But that is an encouragement to us: for all his misunderstanding, lack of faith and poor grasp of vital realities, he *was* called to be a disciple and an apostle—and Jesus never ditched him! He is still there in Acts 1:13, fifth in the list among the apostles, sitting in a prayer meeting and waiting for the Sprit to come so that he could commence a world-wide mission to make disciples of every nation and lay the foundation of the universal church (Ephesians 2:20) to the glory of the Father and the Son—and that is still the role of all God's little people.

Nathaniel Bartholomew— faith with integrity

'Here is a true Israelite, in whom there is nothing false' John 1:47

The name of Bartholomew appears in all the lists of the apostles, but nowhere else, and we are told nothing about him. This would make him unique among the apostles except for one thing: it is very likely that Bartholomew is to be identified with the Nathanael whose call to follow Christ is recorded in the first chapter of John's Gospel. There are a number of very good reasons for this identification. In the first place, 'Bartholomew' is what is called a 'patronym'—a family name describing who his father was; 'bar' means 'son of', so the name literally means 'son of Tolmai'. This would not be an uncommon way of identifying someone, but clearly he would have another, more personal name; it would be tragic to go through life known only as the son of his father! In the Gospels and Acts we have Bartimaeus, Barabbas, Barnabas (a nickname) and Bar Jesus; in two of these instances we are given their alternative name.

A second reason for identifying Bartholomew with Nathanael is that in John 1:45 Nathanael was introduced to Christ by Philip, and in all the Gospel lists of the apostles (Acts 1:13 is an exception), Bartholomew appears next to Philip; clearly these two men were close friends and when you thought of one, you thought of the other. Thirdly, this chapter in John's Gospel is the record of the call of the first apostles, because Andrew, John, Peter and Philip are all there. If Nathanael was not to be an apostle then he would be the odd man out. A fourth reason is that in John 21:1–3, when Jesus revealed himself to some of his disciples by Galilee after his resurrection, Nathanael is listed with Peter, Thomas, James and John 'and two others of his disciples'. If Nathanael was not one of the apostles, then he is misplaced here also. For these reasons, we must either identify Bartholomew with Nathanael or else wonder why we know nothing more about Nathanael other than his call in John 1 and nothing more about

Bartholomew other than that he was one of the Twelve. The first three Gospels never mention Nathanael and John never mentions Bartholomew, another indication that he was known by the two names.

Bartholomew's personal name Nathanael, means 'God has given' and his home town was 'Cana in Galilee' (John 21:2). The exact location of Cana is still uncertain; there are two possible places, one is twenty-two and half miles north of Nazareth and the other is nine and a half miles north-north east of Nazareth. A good supply of water and an abundance of fig trees makes the latter an attractive suggestion, though modern archaeology seems to favour the former; this village would be some twenty miles to the south west of Bethsaida, the home of his friend Philip. Either way, Cana was some distance from Galilee and the only reason that Nathanael the son of Tolmai would be engaged in fishing, which is implied by John 21:1–3) is if he had moved home to be nearer the coast. Perhaps he stayed with Philip in Bethsaida? The only references to the village occur in John's Gospel as the site of the first miracle of Christ (2:1–11), the healing of the nobleman's son (4:46–54), and the home town of Nathanael (21:2).

Legend has played with the subsequent missionary work of Nathanael as with all the apostles. Various accounts send him to Asia, Ethiopia, Egypt, Persia, India, to the shores of the Black Sea and finally Armenia, where he was beheaded, or flayed alive and crucified! Inevitably, there is an apocryphal *Gospel of Bartholomew*. All of which cannot detract from the profoundly simple yet true story given to us in the Gospel of John.

Bartholomew's hope

Nathanael Bartholomew was a faithful Jew, waiting and longing for the coming Messiah. Philip's claim: 'We have found the one Moses wrote about in the Law, and about whom the prophets also wrote—Jesus of Nazareth, the son of Joseph.' (John 1:45) was, as we mentioned in the story of Philip, a most unlikely introduction. The phrase 'Jesus of Nazareth' was hardly calculated to inspire Bartholomew with hope and confidence. Philip claimed to have found the one referred to by Moses and the prophets, and yet nowhere did the Hebrew Scriptures ever make reference to the town of Nazareth either in connection with the Messiah or with anything else; the name does not appear in the Old Testament, and for that matter it did not appear in the *Apocrypha*—a collection of books compiled between Malachi and Matthew—or even later in the history written by the Jewish scholar Josephus, or the writings of the rabbis in the *Talmud*. Besides, Nazareth was situated in a valley, high in the Lebanon range in an area of Lower Galilee, and whilst straddling an important trade route, it was considered to be aloof and independent. It was not so much 'despised' as 'irrelevant' when it came to Messianic expectations.

Nathanael's response was as predictable as it was understandable; there was a certain national pride and religious zeal that prevented him from expecting that the Messiah would come from such an unknown and out of the way place. In Nathanael's mind, the Messiah and Nazareth just did not fit. He had no quarrel with the idea that Moses and the prophets wrote about the Messiah—that fact every faithful Jew believed; we cannot properly understand the Old Testament unless we grasp this essential fact that it is fundamentally about the Christ. This is something that Philip and Nathanael understood better than many Christians.

From Genesis 3:15 onwards, the Old Testament is about God fulfilling his promise to the human race. When he warned the serpent: 'I will put enmity between you and the woman, and between your offspring and hers; he will crush your head, and you will strike his heel', this was not about snakes and men, but about Satan and Christ. From there on, every new development in God's revelation was nudging the human race nearer to the time when 'God sent his Son' (Galatians 4:4). Moses introduced the ceremonials and sacrifices that were pointers to the ultimate 'Lamb of God'; and nine hundred years before Christ was born, David's great Messianic Psalm 22 was a clear marker. Two hundred years later so were Isaiah's prophecies (7:14; 9:6; 53), as were Zechariah's, two hundred years after that (9:9).

There were many more passages in their Hebrew Scriptures that the Jews looked to for fulfilment when the Messiah came.

Nathanael's response was not doubting the possibility of the arrival of the Messiah, but only the place that Nazareth had in that appearance. He had yet to learn that in Christ spending most of his childhood and youth in an irrelevant town like Nazareth, God was already setting an example that he would choose 'the foolish things of the world to shame the wise ... the weak things of the world to shame the strong... the lowly things of this world and the despised things ...' (1 Corinthians 1:27–28). If it seemed strange to Nathanael that the Messiah would come from Nazareth, how much more strange that when he came, he would choose little people like him and his friend Philip to be messengers of the faith!

Philip's reference to 'the son of Joseph' was hardly more helpful for Nathanael Bartholomew. Joseph was unknown on the shores of Galilee, and the fact that Jesus had at least one generation of parentage was scarcely calculated to persuade Nathanael. But perhaps the inclusion of 'Nazareth' and 'son of Joseph' are intended as much for our benefit as for Nathanael's. They are clear marks of an authentic narrative. If, as some critics assume, these records were invented by the church a century or two after the supposed events, why on earth would they conceive, still less include, the idea that Jesus came from Nazareth and that he was the son of Joseph? Any later writer would know that the first was irrelevant and the second was not strictly true. This would hardly support their assertion that Jesus was the long-awaited Messiah, and it would certainly never persuade sceptical Jews. A reference to Bethlehem would have been more in order, since this would provide a valuable link with the birthplace of Israel's great king, David, and it also had the support of the prophet Micah (Micah 5:2). The only possible explanation for the inclusion of Nazareth and Joseph here, is that this is what Philip actually said.

Philip responded with the best possible answer to Nathanael Bartholomew's doubts: 'Come and see' (v 46). That is virtually what Jesus had said to Andrew and John (v 39). A man may spend a lifetime studying the Scriptures until he knows all there is to know about the Messiah, but it will not bring him any nearer membership in the kingdom of God unless he meets Jesus personally. Saul of Tarsus once knew all about the Messiah from his Hebrew Scriptures, and doubtless he had even heard some of the stories of the life and ministry of Jesus of Nazareth, but it was only when he met the Saviour personally that he understood the reality of salvation.

Bartholomew's character

Nathanael received a beautiful character reference from Jesus: 'A true Israelite, in whom there is nothing false' (John 1:47)—and this from the omniscient Lord who 'did not need man's testimony about man, for he knew what was in a man' (John 2:25). 'A true Israelite' refers to the fact that Nathanael was genuine. This was followed by an assertion that in him there was nothing distorted or deceitful. Paul employed the same word to distance himself from those who 'distort the word of God' (2 Corinthians 4:2), and apparently he had been accused by them of the same thing (12:16)—a charge which he strongly rejected (1 Thessalonians 2:3 where the word is translated by 'trick'. It originally referred to a bait or a snare, but gradually it evolved into a reference to deceit or guile).

Clearly, our Lord intended a reference not only to the general character of Nathanael, but to his handling of the Scriptures in their relation to the coming Messiah; he did not criticise Nathanael's caution over Nazareth, on the contrary he commended it. Nathanael was anxious to be guided by the Scriptures and would not lightly accept anything that appeared to be in contradiction of it—that could only bode well for a future apostle. Far from his response being an example of sceptical doubt, it was a commendable instance of biblical caution. Nathanael reasoned that he could not possibly verify the Messiah unless the claimant conformed to the prophecies. And at first hearing, this man from Nazareth certainly did not.

It should be the sincere commitment of every disciple of Christ, that in each part of their life, and particularly in handling the word of God, they are utterly without deceit. To ignore the commands of Scripture, or to twist its clear meaning to suit our own preference is well known to the Master. Paul was able to leave it to the judgement of the Thessalonians to verify that he had never manipulated the word of God to his own advantage: 'We have renounced secret and shameful ways; we do not use deception, nor do we distort the word of God. On the contrary, by setting forth the truth plainly we commend ourselves to every man's conscience in the sight of God' (2 Corinthians 4:2).

Bartholomew's confession

Nathanael Bartholomew was the first person ever to experience a miracle from the Son of God during his earthly ministry. Up to this point, Nathanael had no reason to suppose that Philip or anyone else had been speaking about him with reference to his honest and straightforward character, so, bypassing the obvious compliment, it was natural for him to ask, 'How do you know me?'. The next piece of information convinced him that Jesus was no ordinary man and that he knew everything: 'I saw you while you were still under the fig-tree before Philip called you' (v 48). There is little point in guessing precisely what this refers to; the fact is, we have no idea. Some think it is a metaphorical reference to Nathanael's study of the Scriptures, but this is very doubtful. It was clearly an instance that would immediately jolt his memory to a recent occasion when no one was around and therefore it demonstrated the complete knowledge of this Jesus of Nazareth. This was a lesson that, over the next few years, he and the apostles would learn many times (John 2:24; Mark 9:33–37).

Nathanael was also the first person in the public ministry of Jesus to make a clear confession of who he really was. Unlike the Samaritan woman who, when confronted with the same omniscience could only question: 'Could this be the Christ?' (John 4:29), Nathanael had no doubt, and his response was: 'Rabbi, you are the Son of God; you are the King of Israel' (v 49). 'Rabbi' was a mark of respect that the disciples later changed more frequently to 'Lord'. It is hardly surprising that after his resurrection Jesus is never referred to as 'Rabbi' by the apostles. Mary Magdalene did so only in her momentary confusion (John 20:16).

Significantly, the two claims of Nathanael: 'Son of God' and 'King of Israel' were the two charges that would lead to Jesus' execution. As Son of God he was claiming to be equal with God, and that was a blasphemy worthy of stoning (John 5:18 and 10:29–33). As King of Israel, it was the one and only charge that could genuinely be made against him that might compel Pilate to take action; certainly it was what so infuriated Herod. We often overlook the fact that Peter's confession at Caesarea Philippi: 'You are the Christ, the Son of the living God' (Matthew 16:16), was not a startling new discovery; Nathanael had long before come to this conclusion. He appears to have been the most discerning and fast learning of all the apostles.

Now that Nathanael was so far believing, Jesus encouraged him with the promise that he would experience far greater things; this was to be true not only for Nathanael, but for all the disciples. However, Nathanael's spiritual understanding implied that he would grasp, sooner than most, exactly what Christ had come to do. For the first time we read the strong affirmation by Jesus in the words 'I tell you the truth'. In the original, this is the repetition of the word *amen*, and it was to be a familiar phrase on the lips of Jesus, repeated twenty-six times in the Gospel of John alone. It was our Lord's way of emphasising that his authority did not stem from the Old Testament, still less from the Rabbis; on the contrary, he alone gave the Hebrew Scriptures their authority as its divine author. His words were of sufficient authority and were self-authenticating.

But what did Jesus mean by: 'You believe because I told you I saw you under the fig-tree. You shall see greater things than that. I tell you the truth, you shall see heaven open, and the angels of God ascending and descending on the Son of Man' (John 1:50–51)? Clearly this was a reference to Jacob's dream at Luz (Genesis 28), and that would not be lost on a man of Nathanael's grasp of the Hebrew Scriptures. As such, our Lord was drawing his attention to the fact that over the next three years, Nathanael Bartholomew would see evidence of the kingdom of God as Jacob had done; the detail would unfold as time progressed, but it was sufficient for Nathanael to receive the promise of greater things ahead.

But there was far more to it than this, for our Lord went on to draw a clear comparison with the vision of Daniel (7:13–14), and this would not be lost on Nathanael either. It is interesting that although Nathanael identified Christ as 'Son of God' (John 1:49), Jesus responded by referring to himself as 'Son of Man'. More than eighty times Jesus refers to himself by this title in the four Gospels and here is its very first use. In fact, John 12:34 is the only time it was used by anyone other than Christ himself, and then the crowd were simply mimicking his own phrase. It was clearly a significant phrase for Jesus, and he shared it first with Nathanael the son of Tolmai. For all the miracles and signs that Nathanael would witness, it was vital that he should realise Jesus was not only the Son of God, but also the true Man who had come to redeem his people. He was the Man of sorrows (Isaiah 53:3)—but from heaven. Only as the Son of Man could he fulfil the redemption that he and his Father purposed for the human race.

What were the 'greater things' that Nathanael would see? All that lay before him as an apostle. He would be privileged to witness the Son of Man 'reveal his glory' in countless ways as heaven touched earth over the next three years. In fact, the revelation would begin sooner than Nathanael expected, because within three days he would see the first public miracle of the Son of Man (John 2:1–11).

None of the other apostles was told so much, so early; but then, none of the other apostles understood so much so soon. Their call was mundane compared with that of Bartholomew Nathanael, and if ever there was an example of more being given to those who already have much, he is that example (Luke 19:26). Spiritual wisdom is a gift from God, and the more he gives, if it is used wisely, then the more it will increase. What must amaze us, however, is that from this mountain top understanding of who Christ was, Bartholomew Nathanael seems to have descended, along with all the rest, into the valley of dull doubting as time passed! If he believed so firmly and so quickly with such little evidence before him, how could he possibly not understand the true character of Jesus and his mission as the next few years unfolded? This would be an unsolvable mystery to us if we were not only too aware of our own regular unbelief in the face of such daily evidence of God's grace in our lives.

From this one interview with Jesus, Nathanael passed from the scene and, apart from the apostolic lists and that brief fishing trip in John 21, he is never mentioned again, either as Nathanael or Bartholomew. But he showed a deeper understanding of who Jesus was than any of the apostles at their call, and more was revealed to him than to any of the others. Yet even he was not in the inner circle of three.

James and John—sons of thunder

'James son of Zebedee, and his brother John (to them he gave the name Boanerges, which means Sons of Thunder)' Mark 3:17

Two hot-tempered and explosive brothers lived in Bethsaida at the northern tip of Galilee, and the name of their town revealed the chief occupation: 'the house of fishing'. James was probably the elder of the two because he is almost always mentioned first. Their father was Zebedee (Matthew 10:2), and they worked together in the family fishing business; it was a consortium with Peter and Andrew because Luke 5:10 refers to James and John as 'Simon's partners'; the home of Peter and Andrew at Capernaum was only a few miles away. It would appear to have been a thriving business, and they could afford to hire men during the busy season of fishing (Mark 1:20). Galileans were known to be a hardy and hardworking race, and very committed to Jewish nationalism. The call of these two brothers to follow Christ came at the same time as the call of Andrew and Peter (Mark 1:16–20), and whilst this does not mean that they never fished again (assuming that Luke 5:1–11 is another occasion), the loss of the four leading partners would have placed large demands upon the hired men.

It is very likely that the mother of James and John was the Salome mentioned in the resurrection story recorded in Mark 16:1 ('Mary Magdalene, Mary the mother of James, and Salome' and compare 15:40), because in the same narrative Matthew refers to 'Mary Magdalene, Mary the mother of James and Joseph, and the mother of Zebedee's sons' (Matthew 27:56). Almost certainly, Salome was one of the women who supported Jesus 'out of their own means' (Luke 8:3); but more intriguing is the possibility that she was the sister of Mary, the mother of Jesus. The reason for this is that John 19:25 refers to four women standing near the cross, 'his mother, *his mother's sister*, Mary the mother of Clopas, and Mary of Magdala', whilst Matthew informs us that many women were there including Mary Magdalene, Mary the mother of James and Joseph, and *the mother of Zebedee's sons*' (27:56); Mark 15:40 confirms this.

If, then, 'his mother's sister' is Salome, James and John would be cousins to Jesus. Some have suggested that Salome was the daughter of a priest, and this could explain why John had access to the high priest's courtyard, being known personally to the high priest (John 18:15). This strange fact, mentioned only by John himself, is one of the unsolved mysteries of the Gospels: why should a fisherman from Galilee be personally known to the high priest in Jerusalem unless there was some family link? It is another mark of an authentic record—why would anyone make it up? Fishermen they may be, but they appear to have had contacts in high office and consequently enjoyed a certain social standing in the community.

There are four other James in the New Testament: One is another apostle, who was the son of Alphaeus and brother of Joses, and whom some identify with the son of Mary and nicknamed 'the younger or smaller' (Matthew 10:3 and Mark 15:40). A second James is the brother of Jude (Jude 1) who is almost certainly the brother of our Lord (see Mark 6:3); this James became the leading elder in Jerusalem and the author of the New Testament letter with his name attached (Galatians 1:19, Acts 15:13 and James 1:1). The third James was the father of an apostle called Judas (Thaddaeus), though not Judas Iscariot (Luke 6:16), and the fourth was father of Joseph, the husband of the virgin Mary (Matthew 1:16 where 'Jacob' is the Old Testament equivalent). Similarly there are three other men with the name of John: the first is John the Baptist, the second, John Mark, the son of Mary and a nephew of Barnabas (Acts 12:12), and the third, a relation to Annas the High Priest (Acts 4:6).

The character of these two brothers
John was probably the younger of the two brothers because on four occasions in the Gospels he is described as 'the brother of James', and he seems to be as content with this as he was to be Peter's companion in mission during the early years of the church recorded in Acts. There, it is clearly Peter who, typically, was both spokesman and leader of the two, but

it was both John as well as Peter who were acknowledged for their courage (Acts 4:13).

However, if our Lord had a sense of humour it was shown in his nickname for these brothers: 'to them he gave the name Boanerges, which means Sons of Thunder' (Mark 3:17). Mark is the only Gospel writer to tell us this, and he interprets the Aramaic word for his Greek readers; the Greek verb (*bronto*) certainly means 'to thunder', though some think it might be more accurately translated by 'rage'. It scarcely requires much imagination on our part to appreciate what these two boys were like, and it is all the more ironic since their mother's name, Salome, is taken from the Aramaic *shalom*, meaning peace! Genes are more significant than names in passing on the traits that will be found in our children.

There are two episodes that illustrate the rough natures and explosive characters of these two tough fishermen. Luke 9:54 records the occasion when a certain Samaritan village had rebuffed Jesus, and the two brothers exploded in anger: 'Lord, do you want us to call fire down from heaven to destroy them?' They remembered the story of Elijah in the Old Testament where the prophet saw two successive groups of soldiers killed by fire when they were sent from Ahaziah to arrest him (2 Kings 1:9–12); that story appealed to these two brothers! However, the Lord simply 'rebuked them' and moved on to another village.

Earlier, the disciples had been quarrelling over who would be greatest when Christ came into his kingdom—it is not difficult to guess who were at the centre of such an argument—and Jesus calmed the situation with a lesson on childlike humility. Apparently John was only half listening, because he wanted to gain credits by informing Jesus of a bold action he, and presumably his brother, had taken when they saw a man driving out demons 'in your name'. Hoping for some commendation, John continued: 'We tried to stop him, because he is not one of us' (Luke 9:49). The fact that they 'tried' implies that they failed, and once more John was put firmly in his place by the Lord. However, there is no reason to assume that James and John did not have the highest motives for their action: a love for Christ and a jealous concern for the honour of his work doubtless motivated them. But to do the wrong thing for the right motive does not vindicate our action.

'Be angry, and do not sin' (Ephesians 2:6) is one of Paul's challenging commands in his letters. For the Christian to be indignant, even angry, with a jealous concern for the honour of Jesus Christ in the face of blasphemous ridicule, is commendable—in fact it would be tragic when Christians are no longer angry at sin in any form—but anger must be controlled. For anger to spill over into uncontrolled violence and threats has no place in the Christian gospel. Christianity, unlike many of the world's religions, is essentially peaceful and never condones violence in defense of the truth.

These two young men were irrepressible, and clearly very conceited. They risked the ill-will of the other ten by making a special request of Jesus for preferential treatment in the kingdom of God (Mark 10:35–45). The whole episode is so instructive that we must delay here for a moment. On their way to Jerusalem, Jesus had been preparing the apostles, yet again, for all that lay ahead: his suffering, death and resurrection. James and John must have been more alert that many of the others, since they clearly understood that after death would come glory—and that was their cue. They approached Jesus with a request for special treatment when Christ returned to establish his kingdom: 'Let one of us sit at your right and the other at your left in your glory.' To be fair, when Jesus declined their request but warned them that they, like him, would drink a bitter cup and experience a baptism of fire, they did not back off. They were not cowards—at least, not yet.

When the rest of the apostles got to hear of this request, 'they became indignant with James and John' and once again, our Lord had to give them all a lesson in humility: reminding them that they must be very different from the pride and conceit of the world, and follow the Son of Man who 'did not come to be served, but to serve, and to give his life as a ransom for many' (Mark 10:45). That attitude must govern all relationships in the church. Rewards in heaven there may be, but for any Christian to *demand* them, is foolish and arrogant conceit.

However, on the credit side of these brothers, it was devotion and loyalty that led them to make such a request. Which of his disciples, then or now, would not wish to be close to Jesus in his glory? But that privilege is for the Father to decide. In his letter, James (not this apostle, who had received the martyrs crown by then) urges humility on the disciples of Christ: 'If you harbour bitter envy and selfish ambition in your hearts, do not boast about it or deny the truth ... For where you have envy and selfish ambition, there you find disorder and every evil practice. But the wisdom that comes from heaven is first of all pure; then peace-loving, considerate, submissive, full of mercy and good fruit, impartial and sincere. Peacemakers who sow in peace raise a harvest of righteousness' (James 3:13–18).

Clearly James and John were used to getting their own way, and the ambitious admiration of their mother did nothing to help them. Matthew informs us that their mother was the one who instigated that bold request: 'Then the mother of Zebedee's sons came to Jesus with her sons and, kneeling down, asked a favour of him. "What is it you want?" he asked. She said, "Grant that one of these two sons of mine may sit at your right and the other at your left in your kingdom"' (Matthew 20:20–21). If Salome was one of those women who supported the Lord out of her own means, perhaps she hoped for some consideration in return for it. She was only human, and wanted the best for her sons, but her misplaced request got them both into serious trouble with their colleagues, and showed the family in a less than favourable light. She may fall on her knees in prayer, but just as the boys' right motive did not vindicate their wrong action, so her humble demeanour did not justify a mistaken request. If our prayers are out of line with the will of the Father, we may be very sincere in our attitude and words, but it will not persuade the Master.

There is a distinct sense that these two brothers were always jockeying for power among the apostles. After all, they had been taken into the inner circle of three of our Lord's circle of twelve, and John already felt that the Master has a special affection for him. Perhaps this is what lay behind the episode recorded in Luke 5:10 when, after the miraculous catch of fish, all the disciples were astonished, but Luke adds pointedly: 'and so were James and John, the sons of Zebedee, Simon's partners.' That fact appears noteworthy for Luke; doubtless he heard about it because the disciples often commented on it: 'even James and John were impressed at that'. These two brothers knew how to fish, and fish successfully; they did not need anyone to tell them how to get a good catch on Galilee, least of all a man who had probably never done a day's fishing in his life; what would the son of a village carpenter be expected to know about the fishing industry? Jesus knew how to get through to men like this: he showed them who was in control of creation in general, Galilee in particular, and right now, the fish especially.

Jesus has his own ways of meeting our arrogance and pride. It may not always be as gentle as the way Jesus dealt with these two disciples so, to borrow the words of Paul, 'do not think of yourselves more highly than you ought, but rather think of yourselves with sober judgment, in accordance with the measure of faith God has given you' (see Romans 12:3). Here, Paul plays with the word for 'think' and adds two prefixes that reminds his readers not to 'hyper-think' but to 'think soundly'.

The privileges of these two brothers

In the Gospels, James is never mentioned without his brother and, together with Peter, they formed an inner circle of the apostles. In the home of the synagogue ruler Jairus when his little daughter was raised from death (Mark 5:37), only these three were allowed in. When Jesus stood on the mount in his heavenly glory (Matthew 17:1–2) again, only these three were present. And they alone were close beside him in the Garden of Gethsemane (Matthew 26:37). We will come later to a possible reason for this special relationship.

John is well known as the apostle of love. Five times he refers to himself in his record of the life of Christ as 'the disciple whom Jesus loved'. The first is at the final supper in the upper room (John 13:23), then at the cross when Jesus committed his own mother into his care (19:26), at the tomb when he 'saw and believed' (20:8), as the one who recognised Jesus from the boat in the early morning on Galilee (21:7), and finally on shore, when Peter drew attention to John and asked Jesus what would happen to this man (21:20–21). This expression 'the disciple whom Jesus loved', seems to have been our Lord's deliberate way by which the hardness and cold determination of the thunderous John would itself be melted into love. The phrase carries no suggestion that Jesus loved John more than the others, but simply that this is how John preferred to refer to himself, rather than use his own name.

Significantly, John never referred to himself by name as the author of the Gospel record; he who once wanted a special place beside his Lord in the kingdom, now writes his name out of his own account of the life, death and resurrection of Christ. His Gospel and his three letters are full of love. There are two hundred and thirty-two occasions when the word 'love' is employed in the New Testament—and almost one quarter of them appear in the writing of John. There are twenty-one references to love in John's first epistle alone, exceeded only in the New Testament by his own Gospel.

There have been many suggestions as to who this 'disciple whom Jesus loved' really was. John does not explicitly claim that he is referring to himself; however, it would make little sense for him to be referring to someone else and refrain from identifying them—how would his readers know who he meant? The traditional view that it was John's way of referring to himself in such a way as to magnify the grace of Christ, is by far the most obvious explanation. Clearly John had been invited by Jesus to sit beside him at the Last Supper, and perhaps all the apostles appreciated that there was a growing understanding between Christ and John. But why? In the normal way we would expect Jesus to treat all the apostles equally. Perhaps there was a deeper appreciation in John about just who Jesus was and what he had come to do; he was, together with his brother, convinced that Christ would one day reign 'in glory' (Mark 10:37), long before the others could even grasp the reality that he would soon be leaving them.

Like Nathanael and now John, those who are given the gift of a deeper understanding of spiritual realities, at the same time enjoy a deeper relationship with Christ himself. Our Lord knew only too well the role that John would play in giving the church for all time the revelation of the end time; the book of Revelation belongs to a man who lived very close to Christ and could be trusted to record only what he saw and heard (Revelation 1:9–11)—and that man was John.

The three names closely linked in the apostolic band are the three that come most readily to mind when we are asked to list the twelve apostles: Peter, James and John. These were clearly the inner circle of the Twelve and, as we have seen, often our Lord taught them alone and shared certain privileges with them: they were the only three allowed into the home of Jairus to witness the raising of the synagogue ruler's daughter (Mark 15:37), they alone were with Christ on the Mount of Transfiguration (Matthew 17:1), and it was these three who were drawn apart to be with Christ in his agony in Gethsemane (Mark 14:33). But why this special treatment? Clearly one reason must be that, in line with the demands of the law, our Lord ensured that in some of the most intimate and intense moments in his life, there would always be 'two or three witnesses' (Deuteronomy 19:15).

But there is another reason. Our Lord wanted to train them especially for their particular service in the future and wished to exploit the natural gifts that he had already given them: Peter was undoubtedly a leader among leaders, and would pen two vital letters to the churches as well as provide John Mark with the material for his *Gospel according to Mark*. For his part, John would supply a thoughtful record of the life and teaching of Christ, plus three letters, and was allowed the incredible privilege of seeing things that few men on earth have ever seen—the record of which is inscribed in the last book in the Bible. And James would be the first among the apostles to feel the martyr's sword, and so soon after the church had been formed. It is always possible, of course, that a further reason for bringing these two brothers into the inner circle was that this was the best way to control their arrogant and volatile natures! At least we have evidence by our Lord's example of different levels of training for different types of service.

Two incidents focus on John especially after the arrest of Jesus. He, alone with Peter, returned after all the apostles had deserted Christ in Gethsemane and entered the courtyard of the high priest 'with Jesus' (John 18:15–16). Twice it is recorded that 'the other disciple' was known to the high priest, and it is typical of John to refer to himself in such anonymous terms. Exactly how and why he was known to such an august leader in Jerusalem must remain, as we have already noted, a mystery. In the light of Peter's denial that follows so soon after their admission to the courtyard, it would appear that Peter and John were separated in the melee.

John must always have felt a sense of guilt for gaining permission from the doorkeeper for Peter to join him, but it is intriguing to consider that Peter may have had no need to deny Christ at all, since John was also identified as a follower of Jesus; in fact the girl on duty implied as much when she quizzed Peter: 'Surely you are not *another* of this man's disciples'. John moved freely and was readily known, but no one arrested him.

The other account is that beautiful but brief command of Jesus as he hung on the cross. That it was a tender charge is evident. Near the cross stood a small group of tearful women, including Mary, the mother of Jesus. The only man present appears to be John, 'the disciple whom he loved'. Mary was almost certainly widowed by now and she could expect no support from her other children who at this moment still refused to believe the claims of their brother; Jesus gently gave his mother into the care of John, and 'From that time on, this disciple took her into his home' (John 19:25–27). It says much of the new character of John, that Jesus should entrust his own mother into his care.

The suffering of these two brothers

In reality, the very blemish in the character of these brothers that led Christ to dub them the 'Sons of Thunder', became their strength to face the future that he had marked out for them. If it was later true that Christ would show Paul 'how much he must suffer for my name' (Acts 9:16), it was equally true in the lives of James and John. Jesus had warned them that they would 'drink the cup I drink and be baptised with the baptism I am baptised with' (Mark 10:39), meaning that they would certainly suffer for the sake of the very kingdom they were so eager to share in. It was their strength and forcefulness that was precisely the dogged determination for which the Jewish Sanhedrin reluctantly admired them when Peter and John refused to give up preaching that Jesus had risen from the dead (Acts 4:13). God will certainly use strong and forceful characters, even personalities that can be sharp and at times harsh—but he will only use them for his honour when he has mellowed and moulded them to be 'conformed to the likeness of his Son' (Romans 8:29).

Their misplaced courage and resolution in requesting fire to burn up those who opposed Christ and in ordering a man to stop his work who was not 'one of us', was the same jealous concern for the kingdom that motivated John to stand with Peter on trial and in prison (Acts 4), and for which Paul commended him as one of the pillars in the church (Galatians 2:9). It was the same resolution also that, many years later, encouraged him to pen his three short letters to defend the infant church from the Gnostic errors of his day (see especially 2 John 10–11), and to expose and warn Diotrephes 'who loves to be first'—in whom John must have seen more than a little of his own early characteristics (3 John 9).

There are many natural traits in our character that will hinder the work of the gospel unless Christ brings them into line and converts them for good. We must never make excuses for ourselves and claim: 'That's just how I am and people will have to get used to it.' They do not have to get used to it—we have to change. Until James and John submitted their sharp edges and volatile natures to Christ, they would be dangerous workers in the kingdom of God. But those same weaknesses would become strengths when the Master Potter had remade them.

John passes out of the story of the infant church in Acts after he and Peter had been sent to Samaria to check out the work of Philip (Acts 8); beyond the reference that he was the brother of the James whom Herod 'put to death with the sword' (Acts 12:2) we learn nothing more of him in this record. However, a passing reference by Paul to the welcome he received in Jerusalem from 'James, Peter (*Cephas* is the name used here) and John' (Galatians 2:9) speaks well of his warm spirit of cooperation for the sake of the gospel. Incidentally, the James here must be the brother of our Lord and not the apostle, since John's brother was martyred before Paul came up to Jerusalem on this second occasion, and this is the reason why Luke, in writing Acts, separated James and John by the name of Peter.

John was probably the last of the apostles to enter the kingdom he was so enthusiastic about—so all the seats were allocated before he arrived! However, he did not get there before he had first suffered as an exile on Patmos, a rocky island off the west coast of Asia Minor in the Aegean Sea. Little more than twenty-two square miles in land area, it was hot, windy and, in the first century, few people settled there out of choice. The Roman historian, Tacitus, tells us that the Romans used it as a prison island where they could exile political agitators and anyone else who threatened the peace of Rome. According to the fourth century Christian historian, Eusebius, it was during the time of the Emperor Domitian that John was sent here in the year AD 95; apparently he was released eighteen months later under the elderly emperor Nerva, whose reign was both short and peaceful. A fairly reliable tradition identifies the cave in which John spent much of his time. He may not have been alone, since other Christians were doubtless exiled with him on this 'Robben Island' of the Roman world.

But if John was the last of the apostles to enter into the kingdom, his brother James was the first. The simple statement recorded in Acts 12:1–3 must have sent shock waves throughout the church: 'It was about this time that King Herod arrested some who belonged to the church, intending to persecute them. He had James, the brother of John, put to death with the sword. When he saw that this pleased the Jews, he proceeded to seize Peter also.' Stephen had been martyred largely by mob violence with only a veneer of legality, but James was killed on the official order of Herod Agrippa, the grandson of Herod the Great. The year was AD 44, and this was a major shift in local government policy.

There are the usual cluster of legends that follow James—even after such an early death. The stories of him having preached in Spain prior to his arrest and execution by Herod, and of his body miraculously translated to Compostela in northwest Spain, have given rise to a papal authentication of his relics there, pilgrimages to his sepulchre at Compostela, and an order of Roman Catholic Knights in the twelfth century. As a result of these dubious legends, James is patron saint of Spain! But real history is silent. We know nothing for certain about his movements after Acts 8:1. In reality, James may never have left Jerusalem! The fourth century church historian, Eusebius, certainly believed this was the case, though he does furnish us with a story that he had received from Clement of Alexandria late in the second century, that at his trial before Herod, James' accuser was so moved by his testimony that he became a Christian and died with him.

However, there must have been a reason why Herod chose James as the first victim of his bitterness against the Christians. We can only imagine that it was his determined and forthright character that so upset the Jews and marked him out for their vengeance. He was the first of the apostles to 'drink the cup' that the Master drank. What is interesting for us, is the fact that within the space of a few verses in Acts 12, the Lord allowed James to be killed by the sword of Herod whilst he rescued Peter from prison by the miraculous intervention of angels. The Lord could so easily have rescued James in a similar manner, which helps us to understand that the Lord of the church has different plans for each of his people.

What appears to us as a terrible tragedy when Christians are still today brutally murdered by intolerant religions and governments, will not be seen as a tragedy from the vantage point of heaven. And the miraculous 'escapes' when the invisible angels of God still rescue some of God's servants from danger and death will, from the same view, appear no more or less a gracious act of an all wise, all powerful and all loving God. John would achieve so much: a leader among the churches long after all the other apostles had been martyred, the writer of a deeply thoughtful life of Christ, three valuable letters and the fitting conclusion to the collection of books that make up our Bible. For his part, the legacy of James is nothing more than a life well lived and an early death in obedience to his Master. But will either receive a greater reward in glory? Rewards are for obedience, not achievement.

Following the terrible tsunami on 26 December 2004 that annihilated large areas of coastland by the Indian Ocean and swept almost a quarter of a million people to their death in Indonesia alone, there were many stories of what can only be described as miraculous deliverances for Christians—but thousands of Christians, including entire congregations at worship, were not delivered from the choking clutches of the gigantic waves. The pastor of Zion Church in the coastal town of Bellacore lost thirty three members of his congregation; preaching shortly afterwards he addressed this very problem: members said 'Pastor, some came to Church and died—some stayed at home and died—Why?' He replied 'Let me tell you this message, we are not great enough to even ask God why, just bow to his Almighty ways then he will bless us; he is still a God of mercy even if he speaks at times in ways to compel us to listen.'

John also suffered from a wealth of legends that grew up after his death. One suggests that he was martyred on the same day as his brother (27 December to be precise!). More likely is the very early acceptance that he was alive and living in Ephesus until the days of the emperor Trajan—and Trajan did not begin his reign until AD 98. Here he led the church that he would later encourage for its stiff resolve in the face of false teaching and persecution, but condemn for having lost its earlier love for Christ (Revelation 2:1–4). John probably returned to Ephesus after his brief exile on Patmos, and tradition claims that he died peacefully—the only apostle to whom tradition assigns this privilege!

But there is one story that carries more than a little reality, knowing the man as we now do. It is claimed that as a very old man in Ephesus, when

John had to be carried to church, he could say no more than 'Little children, love one another', claiming that this was the command of the Lord: 'And if this alone be done, it is enough.' Whether that is true or not, it is a fitting conclusion to the life of one of God's little people, the 'son of thunder' whom Christ called, tamed, changed and converted into the apostle of love.

Matthew Levi—the hated traitor

'Jesus … saw a man named Matthew sitting at the tax collector's booth. "Follow me," he told him, and Matthew got up and followed him' Matthew 9:9

Times were changing for Matthew Levi and his colleague Zacchaeus eighty miles south in Jericho. For centuries the Roman taxation system had been fairly modest. One percent, rising occasionally to three percent, was not over burdensome and this was largely in support of the army to maintain the coveted *Pax Romana*. However, gradually the method shifted and Tax Farmers (they were called *publicani*) were employed to gather an increase in taxation. Areas were put up for auction and the Farmers would bid to gain the right to collect taxes for that area. They were normally wealthy citizens, and they paid the government in advance and were then free to recoup their outlay by whatever means was possible. They could collect taxes in either cash or goods, though Rome insisted on payment, up front, in cash. It could, of course, be a risky business, since the Farmer had to assess the economic potential of his area; but, like all risks, he loaded the premium with this in mind.

The system allowed for the Farmers to employ their own 'chief tax collectors' (*architelones*), who in turn used 'tax collectors' (*telones)* to gather in the money. Some had their own toll house or booth and these were known as the *mokhes*—they were hated more than all. The *Authorised Version* is incorrect by consistently translating the word *telones* by 'publicans'; it is not the *publicani* that are in view in the New Testament, but the men who actually collected the taxes. From the words carefully used in the Bible, it would appear that Zacchaeus was an *architelones* (Luke 19:2) and Matthew was a *telones* (Matthew 10:3). He was on the bottom rung of the profession, the man at the coal face, daily in touch with the people, and therefore the immediate object of their bitterness, especially as he was a *mokhes* with his own tax booth. If he had an entrepreneurial spirit and a loose conscience, which almost all had, he could play the system decidedly to his advantage. From Galilee in the north to Judea in the south the tax gatherer was loathed and hated, not only because of his methods of extortion, but because he was working for the occupying power. If he was a Jew, he was a traitor.

But, times were changing. When Augustus came to power in 27 BC he listened to the complaints of the citizens and altered the system. Augustus cut out the Farmers and introduced direct taxation: an income tax of around one percent, plus a tax on produce (ten percent of grain and five percent of wine and fruit) plus a poll tax up to the age of sixty-five on all males over fourteen years and females over twelve; in addition a customs duty was levied on virtually all other commodities, including movement (carts and pack animals) on roads, bridges and the ships in and out of the harbours. To operate all this a regular census of people and property was necessary, and the tax men like Matthew and Zacchaeus, who naturally stayed at their post though now more as inland revenue and customs officers, were directly answerable to central government. They may have stashed away a considerable fortune in 'the good old days' but now there was less room for enterprise. Augustus died in AD 14 and when his son, Tiberius, took over the Empire throughout the adult years of Jesus of Nazareth, the outlook was even more bleak. Tiberius slashed his father's building programmes and hoarded the savings; as a result there was a serious shortage of money in circulation.

Apart from his name appearing in three lists of the twelve apostles, the only other reference to Matthew in the Bible is in the story of his call by Christ, and that story is recorded by Matthew, Mark and Luke. Nowhere in the four Gospel records is Matthew credited with ever saying anything! This is a fact that he shares only with James the Less and Simon the Zealot. For obvious reasons, we will focus on Matthew's own account, though all three are virtually identical. With the exception that Mark and Luke both give us his family name of Levi.

Capernaum was his work base, and it was an important town at the northern end of the Lake of Galilee; it played a significant role in the ministry of our Lord in this area, and almost certainly he made Capernaum his base whilst preaching around Galilee. Not only was it by the lakeside, but it straddled a vital caravan route from the Mediterranean coast (from Caesarea for example) to Syria, and it enjoyed an excellent water supply. With fishing on one side, good fertile agricultural land on the other, and a trade route passing through the centre, it was inevitable that a customs post was situated here and, as a frontier town, a military detachment was stationed here as well. Capernaum was fiercely Judaist in its religion and politics, and it remained so for many centuries to come; there was no love for Gentiles or 'heretics' within its surroundings.

Matthew Levi was no stranger in this significant lakeside town. His custom post or 'toll booth' was a familiar sight, and was certainly well known to the fishermen who had already been called to follow Jesus of Nazareth—they hated its very existence. But they were not alone in detesting this evidence of imperial authority. Although Matthew enjoyed the protection of the local militia, the taxes that he gathered went to Herod who, in turn, passed a substantial proportion to the Emperor's coffers in Rome. That meant that he was in league with the enemy and no one had a good word in defence of tax collectors. According to Jewish law, Matthew Levi was debarred from any religious office, and the Pharisees considered that there were two classes in society for whom repentance was especially difficult: tax gatherers and herdsmen. Money, only money, mattered to him. His shekels were his shackles.

To illustrate their contempt for these people—and the words 'tax collectors' and 'sinners' were synonymous to the Pharisees and most Jews—the rabbis told a story of the son of a pious man who died and the son of a taxman who died: the son of the pious man was carried unmourned to his grave because he had committed one transgression, whilst the son the taxman was carried to his grave amid great honour because he had achieved one good deed! Seaside tax collectors were considered to be especially ruthless and a proverb went the rounds: 'Woe to the ship that sails without having paid its dues.' Matthew's powers were not limited to sitting idly at his custom post waiting for honest folk to arrive with their taxes, he had the authority to search wagons and ships and levy the appropriate dues. As with most governments, the imperial authority found ways to tax just about everything that moved or could be eaten, worn, lived in or ridden. The powers of the *telones* were virtually unlimited and any traveller could be stopped and forced to unpack his baggage for inspection. This was one reason why Matthew needed friends in the military. Rome was always ready to use traitors, even though she never admired them.

By character, by occupation and by reputation, Matthew Levi was effectively shut out from the religion and society of Israel. He had friends of course, but they were all of the same profession. We can easily imagine the shock to the law-abiding fishermen among Jesus' disciples when Matthew Levi joined the team! And if Simon the Zealot, that patriotic pro Israel agitator, had already been called up by Jesus, Matthew joining the recruits must have been a bridge too far. You could hardly have found two men of more opposite loyalties!

A chance to believe

Matthew Levi had seen Jesus often. The crowds that followed him gave hope for some hike in income, but more especially, he had doubtless seen some of the miracles of healing and certainly had heard the reports: the demon possessed delivered, the sick healed, the blind restored, lepers cleansed and a man with total paralysis walking. This was all good news for Matthew—more fit labourers meant more potential taxes. He would be on good terms with the local military, and doubtless knew personally the centurion whose servant had recently been miraculously healed (Matthew 8:5–13). This *telones* was told that even one of his regular 'customers', Peter the fisherman, had seen his wife's mother restored from a dangerous fever (vs 14–17). Besides all this, stories were buzzing around the town as to the reason for the sudden calming of the fierce storm that battered the lake a few nights ago (vs 23–27). If he had not dared to be out on the hillside himself, perhaps snippets of the recent teaching of Jesus from there had been reported to him (chapters 5–7).

If there was one thing that perhaps intrigued Matthew, it was the claim of Jesus to forgive sins. That had been the subject immediately before Matthew's call (9:1–8), but it was not the first time. According to the Pharisees, forgiveness had to be earned—there would be no welcome from

God until a man ceased to be a sinner; and also according to the Pharisees, 'the ignorant cannot be pious'—and piety was a return to the law, not to God. The Pharisees had no idea of a forgiveness that was free; it could only be earned by a life of good works—and on all counts, Matthew Levi was excluded.

How much he had heard, and how much his mind was prepared, we are not told. But the phrase in v 9 'As Jesus went on from there', implies that the healing of the paralysed man took place not far away from Matthew's tax booth and just before Jesus called him. Significantly, the dramatic events of the friends pulling off the roof to lower the man in front of Jesus, are left to Mark to record (Mark 2:1–12). Matthew is usually more concise than Mark, and now he overlooks the excitement of all that and focuses on what clearly impressed him most about the whole episode: not the hole in the roof, but the claim of Jesus to forgive. Matthew must have been aware of the brief discussion between Jesus and the Pharisees when this Rabbi offered supreme hope to the poor man: 'Take heart, son; your sins are forgiven'; after all, the whole town was buzzing with the story (Matthew 9:8). The compassion and authority with which he assured the man of acquittal for his sins would have registered with Matthew, who knew that he was at the bottom of possibilities when it came to forgiveness and salvation. He had betrayed his name and his nation twice over.

Parents then, as now, tended to choose names for their children according to the latest fashion. Matthew was a common name at this time because Mattathias Maccabaeus had launched the Maccabean wars nearly two hundred years earlier which bravely resisted the Syrian oppressors and, as they claimed, 'the yoke of the Gentiles was removed from Israel'. This began an upsurge of Jewish nationalism that was still rife, especially in this part of Galilee. Mattathias Maccabaeus and his five sons were national heroes, and every young boy in Capernaum would know the daring exploits of these great fighters for freedom. Naming their son Matthew, was an act of defiance against the occupying forces. Besides, several High Priests and Rabbis had carried this name, and perhaps his parents hoped he would one day follow a route into the priesthood. They had good reason for this expectation because his family name was Levi, and that revealed to all that this man was from the priestly tribe—as it happens, the same tribe as that heroic Maccabean family. His credentials were good—but his profession was a disaster. With the advent of Rome, the 'yoke of the Gentiles' was back, and 'Matthew the son of Alphaeus' (Mark 2:14) was on the wrong side.

A call to follow Christ

When Matthew went to work that morning 'beside the lake' at Capernaum (Mark 2:13), who knows what was in his mind. Perhaps he had been thinking about his life in the light of what he knew of this powerful preacher from Nazareth; and perhaps the evidence of the healing and forgiveness of the man with paralysis, just across the way, finally convinced him that he needed Christ. What he could never have expected was that when the sun went down on this day, Matthew Levi would be a new man.

His own story of his call is told in just twenty-two words in the Greek. If anything more went between him and the Lord, none of the Gospel writers tells us. Whilst, as we have indicated, Matthew was well aware of Jesus of Nazareth and all that he had been doing and teaching in the locality, the strong implication is that on this occasion, all we are told is all that happened. Christ came by, paused, looked at Matthew and spoke briefly—nothing more was needed. It was the same powerful and persuasive voice and face that had held back the murderous hands at Nazareth (Luke 4:30), that had stilled the violent storm (Matthew 8:26), and that would one day compel those who came to arrest him to grovel in the dust (John 18:6). Unlike the religious leaders of his day, Jesus of Nazareth was welcoming, reassuring and above all, forgiving. Matthew had seen him and heard him often on the shore and around the town, he knew well some of those who had already joined the close band who followed Jesus—they were his regular 'customers'—but now it was his turn to respond.

Just two words from Christ were sufficient: 'Follow me'. Whatever went through Matthew's mind in that moment, we shall have to wait until eternity to discover; but what we do know is that Matthew was convinced and changed. Luke adds that 'Levi got up, left everything and followed him' (Luke 5:28). This was not a chance passing on the part of Jesus; as with the call of all his disciples, he knew precisely who he would call today—and had planned the place and time from eternity. When Christ calls, determined to save, no one can stand against him. We may not think that *our* call to discipleship was so dramatic or instant, but in fact it was: however long or short the period of preparation, one moment we were a hell-bound sinner, and the next moment we were a disciple of Christ. The circumstances may have been very different, but the result was the same. This effective call from Christ comes, sooner or later, to all who have been 'appointed for eternal life' (Acts 14:38). Too many Christians argue about that truth, but Matthew didn't—he simply followed the irresistible call of Christ.

The story of Matthew's call perfectly illustrates what Jesus meant when he informed the Pharisees: 'I have not come to call the righteous, but sinners' (Matthew 8:13). He was not referring to a call to repentance—even the Pharisees could offer that, though there was little enough hope for a tax collector as we have seen—but it was a call to discipleship. The call was 'follow *me*', and in that same act Matthew would acknowledge that he was living on the wrong side and would therefore turn from his old way of life. Unless the Pharisees understood this, they—who felt so secure in their religion—would perish.

A clear conversion

It is perhaps surprising that, in his record of the life of Christ, Matthew makes no mention of the conversion of that other tax collector, Zacchaeus, down south in Jericho (Luke 19:1–10). There is no reason why he should have known him, but later the story must have come to his attention; and there are similarities in their experience, not least in the meal that each immediately shared with the Man who had so radically changed their lives. Two honest tax collectors in Galilee and Judea must have been something of a novelty!

Whether Matthew 'left everything' (a point that only Luke mentions) permanently or only for a while, we cannot know; after all, the fishermen among the disciples later went back to their trade as a means of at least temporary support. Leaving everything was an immediate decision to follow Christ—and to follow him now. Christ calls every disciple to the same total commitment, though it may work out in a thousand different ways peculiar to each person's circumstances. The Gadarene madman who was healed by Christ wanted to join the band of disciples, but he was told to 'go home' and share the good news of what God had done for him; that was to be his full commitment. On the other hand, when a rich young man made a similar request, the instruction he received was to sell all that he had and give to the poor. Neither command is intended for all in every circumstance; Christ deals with each of his prospective disciples individually. If Matthew did leave his tax collecting for ever, there would be no shortage of men to take his place; however, the 'collectors of the two-drachma tax' referred to in Matthew 17:24 would not be his successors because that was the temple tax, and Matthew was never involved in that trade.

Whereas Christ invited himself into the home of Zacchaeus, it is clear that Matthew took the initiative in throwing a 'great banquet' to which a 'large crowd' was invited (Luke 5:29). This crowd of guests included many tax collectors and sinners (Mark 2:15), which well illustrates the kind of company Matthew normally kept at his table. The other disciples of Jesus were also there, and the whole company must have been something of a steep learning curve for them; who else would be invited to join this inner circle of Christ's followers?

Unless Christ is brought into our home, as well as our business life, then there is no reality in our profession of discipleship. The converted nineteenth century Traveller, Gipsy Smith, commented that Matthew never did a wiser or nobler thing than when he took Christ home. Matthew made no public profession about the change in his life, unlike the clear commitment of Zacchaeus to repay those he had defrauded with interest, but it is inconceivable that the Christ whose power so convinced him, would not also have deeply convicted him. Inviting all his friends to a meal to hear Jesus was a massive testimony in itself. Joseph of Arimathea and Nicodemus remained as secret disciples for some time, but Matthew Levi immediately opened his home to Christ for all to see.

At least the very fact that the crowds would have watched with amazement as he 'left everything' to follow Christ, was a sufficient testimony in itself. Besides, this banquet was not intended to feed Jesus, but for his friends to hear Jesus. Andrew brought his brother Simon, and Philip brought his friend Nathaniel to meet Jesus, but Matthew invited a large congregation to meet the Man who from now on would be first in his life. Much has been said and written on the subject of evangelistic meals, and we can find examples of them in the Gospel records: in the homes of Zacchaeus, Simon the leper and Lazarus and his sisters for example.

There is a simple humility in the way Matthew records this story, so many years after the event. Not only does he dismiss it briefly, but he refused to use his priestly family name 'Levi' and left it to Mark and Luke to add that detail; however, when listing the names of the Twelve he does add significantly: 'Matthew the tax collector' (Matthew 10:3)—as if he wanted people to know what he had once been so that the grace of Christ in calling such a man into his company would be clearly understood. In a similar way, Paul referred often to his past, not boastfully, but as an illustration of God's grace: 'I was once a blasphemer and persecutor and a violent man' (1 Timothy 1:13). Paul never lost sight of the fact that the treasure of the gospel was committed to little people who were no more than 'jars of clay' (2 Corinthians 4:7)—what one preacher calls 'the equivalent of plastic bags'.

And grace it was: the conversion of such a character that the Pharisees had no idea it could happen. Although the guests may have been 'coming and going' in a relaxed manner, it is an indication of Matthew's wealth that his home was sufficiently large to accommodate such a gathering. For their part, the Pharisees who assembled outside were clearly not invited, and had they been, they would not have come; they would have made themselves ritually unclean if they mingled with this lot! In fact Jesus made himself unclean by eating with such people. As soon as they had access to the disciples, the Pharisees demanded to know why Jesus, who many had been calling 'Rabbi', should lower and soil himself in such company. The disciples were too new to all this to have a ready answer, and some may have been thinking the same thing! So Jesus, overhearing the challenge, answered in a simple statement that has become part of our English idioms: 'It is not the healthy who need a doctor, but the sick' (Matthew 9:12).

This was a neat response. They were accusing Jesus, and therefore his disciples, of being contaminated by contact with such a rabble of sinners. In response, our Lord reminded them that in order to heal his patients, even the physician has to get close to them. By eating in Matthew's home with such a crowd of sinners, this great Physician was doing no more than healing the sick! There could be no answer to that. The Pharisees could appreciate the words, but perhaps the meaning was lost on them. So Jesus gave them a short lesson in interpreting the Hebrew Scriptures. The church must be prepared to get close to all kinds of people if they are to be won for Christ.

Jesus' quotation, recorded in v 13, is from Hosea 6:6, 'I desire mercy, and not sacrifice' but it was preceded by a fairly abrupt challenge to go and read their Scriptures with understanding. Right here was their opportunity to put that command into practice. More important than all their ritual and priestly offerings was the fact that a group of social outcasts were listening to the story of one man's changed life, and that opened the door to many more finding salvation. Like the Pharisees, reading our Bible is of little use if we do not discipline our minds to understand it, and our hearts to be obedient.

What shocked the people in the story of Zacchaeus was the claim of Jesus that this man was 'a son of Abraham' (Luke 19:9). In the eyes of the Pharisees, that could never be. People like him were beyond salvation and had no claim to the heritage of Israel. That is precisely what they were thinking in Capernaum about Matthew and his friends. For those who believe that anyone is too bad for God to change and too evil for Christ to save, the words 'Go and learn' ring down the centuries; God himself is the supreme example of mercy, and Christ the supreme example of sacrifice, and those two facts are sufficiently powerful to save all and any.

Christ had come 'not to call the righteous, but sinners to repentance' (9:13 and compare Luke 5:32). This was not intended as a 'let out' for the Pharisees. Our Lord was not suggesting for one moment that they were 'the righteous'; far from it, because he has already condemned them from the prophet Hosea, and elsewhere he rounds on them for their hypocrisy (Matthew 15:7; 22:18; 23:13). What Jesus is clearly implying here is that if they considered themselves too righteous to need repentance and forgiveness, then so be it; he had nothing more to say to people like this until they faced their own sin honestly. It was all so clear in the story of the woman taken in adultery (John 8:3–11). There he would challenge those without sin to throw the first stone at her, and their very silence admitted their guilt.

Matthew's legacy to the church

Beyond the record of the Bible we have little fact and plenty of legend to inform us about the later career of Matthew. The next few years his life were bound up with the other apostles and he would have taken his share of proclaiming and suffering for the good news. It is variously claimed that he gave the Jews the story of Jesus by translating his Gospel into Hebrew, that he travelled to Asia or Persia or Greece or Syria and that he was burned, stoned or beheaded and that he produced many more writings, or none!

What we do know, however, is that well before the turn of the second century all the church leaders are in full agreement that Matthew wrote his gospel, at first in Hebrew for the Jews. Nowhere does the book claim to come from Matthew's hand, and that would be the only certain evidence we have for his authorship. But the early Christian leaders believed it was his, and no other serious claimant has ever been put forward; there is no record of any copy circulating without Matthew's name to it. By the year AD 125 this record was accepted, without challenge, as coming from the hand of Matthew Levi. There is a neat hint of this tax collector's past in the record of the challenge to Jesus by the Pharisees: 'Is it right to pay taxes to Caesar or not?' (Matthew 22:17). In response, Mark and Luke use the word *denarius* when Jesus asked them to bring him a coin; this is correct since the denarius was the coin used for the poll tax. However, Matthew is more precise and refers to it by two words which mean 'census coin' (v 19); he would be only too familiar with this particular currency!

As one who was used to keeping accounts, and possibly using a form of shorthand, Matthew would be a natural choice to record the life and teaching of Jesus. One New Testament scholar has described this Gospel as the product of 'an astonishingly orderly mind', and that is what we might expect of this converted accountant. This, then, was his abiding legacy. So thrilled was he for what Christ had done in his life, and in the lives of so many others, that he must tell the world of this story. With the promised aid of the Holy Spirit who, 'Will teach you all things and will remind you of everything I have said to you ' (John 14:26), Matthew has left us this Gospel record.

There are a number of features of Matthew's Gospel that are his particular emphasis compared with the other three: clearly he views Christ as King and Sovereign, who one day will return with 'power and great glory' and meanwhile calls all men to his side; Matthew is the only Gospel to introduce us to the word *ecclesia* to describe the church, and more than all the others he is particularly interested in what will happen at the end of the age, for which he provides more detail of Jesus' teaching on this subject than any of the others.

However, there is one feature of his Gospel that is of particular interest to us in the light of his own story. Matthew is especially interested in the fact that the message of Jesus reached across the borders of Israel; for him the glory of the gospel is that it is universal. It is Matthew who recounts the story of the Magi from a distant land at the nativity of Jesus (2:1 on), and the brief exile in Egypt of Mary and Joseph with their child (2:13 on). Matthew, along with Mark, could not overlook our Lord's foray into the territory of the Phoenicians (15:21 on), and in the parable of the vineyard it is clear that the kingdom of God will be taken away from Israel and passed to 'a people who will produce its fruit' (21:43), a point which so infuriated the Jews that they immediately planned Jesus' arrest. Finally Matthew records the universal commission given by Christ to his disciples (28:18–20). From his own background as an outcast from Israel—a tax collector was worse, far worse, than a Gentile—Matthew appreciated the universal scope of the message of Christ's kingdom; it opened the door of hope to so many like himself.

Looking at the lives of the twelve apostles, we may be surprised at their very low class backgrounds and, with a couple of exceptions, how little we are told about them. We now know all there is to tell, this side of heaven, about Matthew Levi, the tax collector. But that is so encouraging. We thought them to be such big names, large characters with great achievements, whereas in reality, they are just like us: little people who were chosen and called to discipleship, and in their little way left a legacy of eternal value—and we can all do that.

Simon—the 'dagger man'

'Simon the Zealot and Judas Iscariot, who betrayed [Jesus]'
Matthew 10:4

S imon was a favourite name among the Jews, and the most common name for men in first century Galilee and Palestine. There are seven Simons in the Gospels and two more in Acts so, unsurprisingly, they are normally distinguished by some further identification: there is 'Simon, who is called Peter' and 'Simon of Cyrene' and 'Simon the leper'. Only one word introduces our Simon to us: he is called the 'zealot'. That could mean simply that he was zealous in his character and temperament, in which case it would be a good commendation. Paul describes himself, prior to his conversion, in this way on at least two occasions: 'I was zealous for God' and 'extremely zealous for the traditions of my fathers' (Acts 22:3 and Galatians 1:14). The Greek word *zelotes*, used for Simon in Luke 6:14 and Acts 1:13, refers to someone who is wholehearted and enthusiastic.

However, both Matthew and Mark (Matthew 10:4 and Mark 3:18) employ a different word to introduce Simon to us; they refer to him by the Aramaic word *Kananaios*, 'the Cananean' (The NIV obscures this by the erroneous translation of 'the Zealot'). It does not mean that he came from Cana or Canaan, it is an Aramaic word similar to the Greek *zelotes*, but it was the common reference to a Jewish sect of radicals: after the Pharisees, Sadducees and Essenes, came the Zealots—the Cananeans. Our Simon is mentioned in just three verses in the Gospels and one in Acts, and these four references are nothing more than the lists of the twelve apostles. We are not told of anything that Simon did specifically, or anything that he said. All we know is that his allegiance, before his call by Christ, was to the Jewish party of Zealots.

In the story of Matthew Levi we referred to the heroic struggle of the Maccabeans against the Syrians and then the Romans. After their decisive defeat by the Romans in 100 BC, strong nationalistic sympathies simmered for years and came to the boil in AD 6. In that year, the Roman Procurator, Sulpicius Quirinius, ordered a census to be taken in order to levy taxes on the

Jewish nation. This was among the many reforms by Caesar Augustus, who boasted that he had 'found Rome brick and left it marble'. Overall he was a good and wise emperor, promoting peace and prosperity, with strong internal and external security. *Pax Romana*, the peace of Rome, became a reality.

But the census in Palestine was a step too far for the simmering nationalism of the Jews, because for many, to pay taxes to a pagan emperor was treason to God, who alone was King of Israel. In that year, AD 6, Judas the Galilean raised an insurgency against Rome—it was a revival of the old Maccabean uprising, and its homeland was Galilee. Judas' father, Ezekias, had been executed by Herod for his extreme nationalism, and now his son took up the cause. Those who joined him were referred to as the 'zealous' (*Kananaioi*), because of their zeal for the honour of God. Historically, their fanaticism was linked partly to the zeal of Phinehas, the son of Aaron, in the Old Testament, where the Hebrew word *quana* describes his fervour for the honour of God (Numbers 25:11 and Psalm 106:30–31), and partly because they were taking up the sword from the hand of Mattathias the Maccabean and his five sons. The revolt of Judas the Galilean was brutally crushed in the way that the Romans knew best, and Gamaliel referred to this in his advice to the Sanhedrin recorded in Acts 5:37. The Jewish historian, Josephus, also refers to it. But for sixty years after the crushing defeat of Judas the Galilean and his Zealots in AD 6, the spirit of nationalism was kept alive by the remnants of the party. They were scattered but not cowed.

Two of the sons of Judas the Galilean continued the struggle until they were captured and crucified by the Romans in AD 46, but the third son was still fighting two decades later. The final siege and destruction of Jerusalem by the Roman army in AD 70 was preceded by a civil war in the city instigated by the Zealots, which left over twelve thousand slaughtered; in fact, but for the Zealots' aggressive and brutal behaviour, there probably would have been no siege or destruction of Jerusalem. The Romans stood by and decided to 'allow them, like wild beasts, to tear each other to pieces in their dens.' Josephus describes in detail the callous brutality of the Zealots who, in their utterly misplaced passion: 'trampled upon all the laws of men, and laughed at the laws of God', refusing even to allow the heaps of dead to be buried. Weakened by their self-inflicted carnage, and after a terrible siege, the city finally fell to the Romans, and the Zealots were driven from town to town until they eventually fled to the hill top fortress of Masada where they made their historic last stand. By May AD 74, when Masada was ultimately stormed and the Romans were met by the eerie silence of hundreds of dead bodies as a result of their suicide pact, the Zealots were a spent force and their cause never recovered.

Somewhere along this short history of the Zealots fits our man Simon, who was called to be a disciple and apostle of Christ, and who, but for the call of Christ, may well have ended his life in that terrible suicide pact on Masada. Before Simon met with Christ, what was his philosophy, the driving force of his life, his values and purpose? The Zealots had much in common with the Pharisees in their commitment to the Old Testament law, but they were driven by a passion for liberty from foreign rulers, with God as their only sovereign and Lord. They did not fear death for themselves, their friends or their family in pursuit of this liberty. To achieve their great goal, the Zealots slowly became a brutal, fearless terrorist movement within Palestine; they were passionately nationalistic, and armed themselves with concealed daggers which they did not hesitate to use on those they regarded as enemies of the Jewish nation. They were known as the 'dagger men' or 'assassins'. To a man like this, Jesus came early in his ministry and, somewhere at sometime, called him to be his disciple. And that call, radically changed Simon's life.

Simon learned to serve a new King

Simon had always served God as his king; in fact, that is what motivated him for all his hatred and dagger work. At this very time, close to the far northern frontiers of the empire, another Jew was serving God as zealously, though in a different manner—but just as ignorantly. Saul of Tarsus was not a Zealot, because he belonged to the party of the Pharisees, but he was equally passionate for the religion and nationhood of Israel. His testimony could have been that of Simon himself: 'A Hebrew of Hebrews; in regard to the law, a Pharisee; as for zeal, persecuting the church; as for legalistic righteousness, faultless' (Philippians 3:5). But like Saul, Simon's fanaticism was without true knowledge, he acted ignorantly of the truth (1 Timothy 1:13). Saul's time to meet with Christ lay still a few years ahead, but Simon's time was now.

From a human point of view, Christ took an incredible risk in calling Simon! Fishermen were pretty harmless and not greatly political. But this man was dangerous: perhaps the military were already on to his number and were only waiting for the opportunity to pounce. Simon was a visionary whose religious, political and nationalistic philosophy consumed him. What if he could never be shaken from his violent determination to rid Israel of Rome? What if his political ideals could never be rooted out of his heart and mind? But then, Christ took an equally foolish risk by calling little people like us to be his disciples—or did he? He knows full well what he can do with every man or woman whom he calls out of darkness into his marvellous light. He makes no mistakes when he makes disciples.

The God Simon had served ignorantly, Christ now revealed to him. Little by little this converted terrorist would realise just who had called him into his service, until the day when, like Thomas, he would be able to call Jesus of Nazareth 'My Lord, and my God.' It would take another three years before Simon and his colleagues understood that 'Anyone who has seen me [Christ] has seen the Father' (John 14:9). But if he ever thought of Christ as a leader in rebellion against Rome, he would soon be disabused. He would learn that this man, who was creator of the world and the universes beyond, was also the most humble man on earth, using his power never for his own benefit—which is the true meaning of the phrase 'something to be grasped' in Philippians 2:6—but only for the purpose of his mission.

There could be no going back for Simon the Zealot, just as there could be no going back for Matthew the tax collector. Christ never offered himself to his disciples as Saviour and friend, with the added option that subsequently they might consider taking him as Lord also. His message from the start was clear: 'If anyone would come after me, he must deny himself and take up his cross and follow me. For whoever wants to save his life will lose it, but whoever loses his life for me will find it. What good will it be for a man if he gains the whole world, yet forfeits his soul?' (Matthew 16:25). Simon did not want the world, only Israel for the Jews, but even that was not to be allowed to stand in the way of obedience to his new Lord and King. Whatever our ambition, our overriding goal in life, it has to be given to the rule of Christ: political philosophy, national pride, religious enthusiasm, personal ambition, even our fanaticism for sport, all must fall before Christ the King.

Simon learned to serve his new King in a new kingdom

From now on, Simon must lay aside his passion for liberty in this world and look for and preach a new kind of liberty in a new kind of kingdom. The sword and dagger must be replaced with sandals and scroll. This was a kingdom whose servants do not fight to maintain it. This was the liberty of forgiveness that Jesus spoke about so often, and the peace was not home rule for Israel, but Christ's rule in our lives. Until now, Simon schemed and fought for self rule for a plot of land some one hundred and thirty miles long and thirty wide. From now on he would submit all his energy and zeal to extend the borders of a kingdom that would reach to the uttermost parts of the earth and that would last for eternity. The kingdom he had long fought for was never quite realised, but this one was 'near' (Matthew 10:7), in fact, it was already among them. Who, in his right mind, would not willingly make that exchange?

For years Simon had been plotting and fighting for freedom, but it had always been so elusive; perhaps a little success here and there, but always the Romans were still in the land. In Simon's mind, freedom would only be realised when the Romans were gone. But when Simon found his true freedom, the Romans were still firmly in the land! He had come face to face with the Man who claimed, 'If the Son sets you free, you will be free indeed' (John 8:36). Suddenly, all his ambitions, values and ideologies seemed so petty and trivial compared to the new life—for time and eternity—that he was receiving from Jesus, the Son of God. This is true of all who are called by Christ: whatever our ambitions and philosophy of life, whatever our goals and values, he changes them all and lifts us from the small minded dreams of this world to something far more important and lasting. Our eyes become fixed on eternity and all that God has planned for us, which is the only lasting reality that we will ever know.

When Jesus later declared: 'Give to Caesar what is Caesar's, and to God what is God's' (Matthew 22:21) that must have made even the converted Simon wince; he had been prepared to shed his blood to deny Rome anything—especially taxes. But now all that was past and he understood the true meaning of giving to God what belonged to him. Some courses in life can be maintained after we come to Christ in faith—it was not wrong for the other Simon and his colleagues to go fishing again—but some cannot. For Simon the Zealot, there had to be a complete break with the past; there was no more room in the kingdom of God for a terrorist in the first century than there is in the twenty-first.

The kingdom of God does not make everything here irrelevant, but it does bring everything into a new light. Simon would still be a citizen in an earthly kingdom—and whether he liked it or not it was Roman. But the kingdom he had been fighting for was so elusive. For centuries, Jews loyal to what they thought was God's covenant with Israel, had fought and died for a small plot of land that somehow they could never hold for long; at last, Simon was beginning to learn of 'a city with foundations, whose architect and builder is God' (Hebrews 11:10).

Simon must have listened with greater attention than any of the disciples to the teaching of Christ about the kingdom. It was the theme of John the Baptist's teaching, and so many of Jesus' parables concerned the 'kingdom of heaven' or the 'kingdom of God'. He encouraged the disciples that the kingdom is 'among you', 'near you', 'upon you', and 'given to you', and sent them out to preach 'good news of the kingdom'. Simon's new Master encouraged him with the 'inheritance of the kingdom' and finally gave to his disciples 'the keys of the kingdom'. But there was a reality and a certainty about this kingdom that was inescapable; and at the end, Christ would return to bring his followers into this kingdom, in all its completeness, to enjoy it with him for ever.

Simon learned to serve his new King in a new kingdom with a new strategy

If Simon's message that he was now preaching had changed to 'the kingdom of heaven is near' (Matthew 10:7), so had his strategy. Now he would go out to 'Heal the sick, raise the dead, cleanse those who have leprosy, drive out demons' (v 8) because: 'Freely you have received, freely give.' The approach now was not demanding the blood of traitors and the death of Romans, but it was about peace and reconciliation, first to God and then to men; no longer was he to drive out Romans, but demons— though Simon had up until now equated the two. When Jesus sent out his disciples as 'sheep among wolves' and instructed them to be 'as innocent as doves' (Matthew 10:16), Simon had never thought of himself as a sheep or dove before; wolf yes, but not a dove.

But to achieve this, Simon's new King demanded that he must hand over his sword—literally—together with his ambitions and values; Christ had plans to renew them all. He would no longer be an assassin, a 'dagger man', but a preacher of the kingdom of God. He must exchange his fanatical nationalism for enthusiastic evangelism. Just as the fishermen were told that they would become 'fishers of men' (Matthew 4:19), so Simon would wield the 'sword of the Spirit, which is the word of God.' (Ephesians 6:17), and would 'demolish strongholds', take 'captives for Christ' (2 Corinthians 10:4–5), and be led in 'triumphal procession in Christ' (2 Corinthians 2:14). The metaphors can always shift from the life behind us to the task before us!

Simon had three years to unlearn his old strategy and become accustomed to the way of spreading the message of this new kingdom. Sharing the message of the kingdom of God by word of mouth and the backup of a quality life, may have appeared tame compared with his old habits, but once Simon had understood the value and values of the kingdom, he could easily appreciate the effectiveness of the method—crowds were following and many lives were being changed.

However, we can sense that all his old nationalistic instincts were awakened when our Lord, three years later, set a little trap for the apostles to test their understanding. It was shortly before Gethsemane, and Jesus was preparing them for the traumatic hours that lay ahead. He first reminded them that he had sent them out without 'purse, bag or sandals' and asked if they had lacked anything. They admitted that all their needs had always been met. The next statement was highly significant: 'But now if you have a purse, take it, and also a bag; and if you don't have a sword, sell your cloak and buy one' (Luke 22:36). The introduction of that word 'sword' was deliberate.

If the disciples had been learning over the past three years, and if they were listening now, they should have responded: 'You don't mean a sword, do you? You mean sandals?' That, after all, was the word Jesus had used in the previous trio: 'purse, bag or sandals'. But they walked into the trap by counting up their hardware and enthusiastically offering: 'See, Lord, here are two swords.' Our Lord's response 'That is enough' meant simply: 'If you think that is the way my kingdom will spread in the future, then two swords will be sufficient because that way will fail however many you have.' And so it was, whenever, in future centuries, the institution called 'church' took to the sword to extend its borders, it was never the kingdom of God that was extended but the empires of men. Any religion or set of beliefs that advocates violence to defend or extend its cause, is a lie and deceit and reveals plainly that it is not on the side of truth.

But where did these two swords come from that the disciples offered to Jesus? One certainly belonged to Peter because he was the one who used it in Gethsemane (John 18:10); but did the other belong to Simon the Zealot who, sensing the dangers of the hour, reverted to his old habits and armed himself? Or had he long kept this weapon hidden because he had broken faith with the party to whom he had once sworn allegiance and he felt it wise to keep a small sword by him 'just in case'? Either way, it was an indictment of all the disciples that at the very end, they failed the test and forgot the nature of the kingdom and its method of extension. It is all too easy for members of the kingdom of God to think that they can extend or defend it by methods more familiar to the powers of the world than the Spirit of God. We are often too slow to break with our past. Our chief strategy for evangelizing the world and defeating unbelief is by the word of God and the power of the Holy Spirit; that, according to Peter, is all that we need for life and godliness (2 Peter 1:3–4). Any religion, whatever its name, that attempts to spread by the force of the sword, proves itself to be on the side of the devil and not of God.

Simon learned to serve his new King in a new kingdom with a new strategy among a new community

We cannot be sure whether Simon was called by Christ before Matthew Levi or afterwards. It hardly matters either way, but what is incredible is to imagine these two men, not only in the same company at any time, but now on the same side! On the one hand a proud, ruthless, nationalistic terrorist, determined to achieve Israel's independence at any cost, and on the other hand, a mean, grasping money-making traitor who was prepared to bear the tag of collaborator and work for the army of occupation, just so long as he could rake in the shekels. These two men had nothing in common. But more than this, Simon hated Matthew with good reason, and Matthew feared Simon, again with good reason. But the Lion of Judah (Revelation 5:5) had tamed two snarling and fighting bears. No one else in first century Palestine could have brought these two men onto the same side in such harmony. This fact seems not to be lost on Matthew who probably took great delight in describing himself as 'the tax collector' and then almost immediately list 'Simon the Zealot' (Matthew 10:3–4)—which is another reason why this designation almost certainly refers to the sect he belonged to rather than his natural temperament. But how did Christ change these men so radically?

Clearly Jesus had shown both men that whatever their cause, their heart was bad. Repentance and therefore forgiveness had come into their lives; and repentance and forgiveness is always followed by reconciliation. These are the indivisible three in the New Testament; they are always found together, never one without the others: repentance, forgiveness and reconciliation. But in forgiving them, Christ replaced their values and goals with something far more stable and strong. The kingdom of God was not just a cause to which they could now turn their attention, it was within them (Luke 17:21); they were part of the kingdom of God and, though they did not fully grasp any of this, they were new citizens of this kingdom. All divisions had broken down and all barriers had fallen away. The most unlikely contrasts were now in harmony.

Tom Kelly had been a sniper with the Irish Republican Army and James Tate had been an Ulster Volunteer Force commander; like Simon and Matthew, the two men were on opposite sides of a bitter struggle. Given the opportunity, Tom would have gladly shot James just as Simon would certainly have driven his concealed dagger into the back of Matthew the traitor. Kelly and Tate came to Christ somewhat differently than Simon and Matthew. They were both arrested, tried and sent to the infamous Long Kesh prison in Northern Ireland. On release, each came to faith in Christ, teamed up and worked together for peace and reconciliation across the nation. That is precisely what happened to Simon and Matthew. When they teamed up with Christ, they teamed up together—and their message was one of peace and reconciliation, first to God and then to men. Years later, when Paul wrote to the church at Ephesus, he admired the way God had brought such a mixture of people together in one body, the church—Jews committed to the law of God, and pagans committed to the temple of Diana, philosophers and hedonists, rich and poor, bankers and merchants, slave and free. The way it happened Paul described like this:

'[Christ] himself is our peace, who has made the two one and has destroyed the barrier, the dividing wall of hostility, by abolishing in his flesh the law with its commandments and regulations. His purpose was to create in himself one new man out of the two, thus making peace, and in this one body to reconcile both of them to God through the cross, by which he put to death their hostility. He came and preached peace to you who were far away and peace to those who were near. For through him we both have access to the Father by one Spirit' (Ephesians 2:14–18).

Simon and Matthew would not grasp all this yet, but they were certainly experiencing more than they could understand. The law-abiding fishermen, who formed the largest group among the apostles, must have been bewildered by the speed with which Jesus brought the most unsuitable and unlikely men into the inner circle. But then, he specialised in doing that, and he still does. It was intended as an example then of what he would do throughout the history of the church. All of which makes the petty quarrels, that so regularly divide our churches today, appear so small-minded in the light of what Christ did when he brought these two men into the kingdom.

Finally

As with all the apostles, there are plenty of legends to choose from when Simon leaves the pages of biblical history. We are told that he preached in North Africa and even here in Britain. In Britain he was crucified by the Romans at Caistor in Lincolnshire and buried there in May AD 61 (or AD 74)—providing you do not accept the legend that he left Britain and went to Persia where he was martyred by being sawn in two! But whatever the truth behind these tales, we could close with a little supposition to more purpose.

Suppose for a moment that we do not know the account of the final week in the life of our Lord, and we have been asked, with all the information gleaned through the gospel story so far, to decide which of the twelve apostles will ultimately betray their Master. Who would we choose? As in all good murder plots where the most unlikely becomes the most likely, we might go for Peter the bold protester of loyalty, or even John, the one specially loved by Christ. We are not yet in the last week, remember, so we have not learned of the deceit of Judas who stole from the common purse (John 12:6), and there is little to direct suspicion towards him.

Simon is surely the most obvious choice: before his call, his whole life had been consumed by a passion to fight for an earthly kingdom, and perhaps he had never been persuaded by the talk of an unseen kingdom that could include even traitors and Romans, and of which the better part would never be realised on this earth as we know it. He of all apostles had reason to despair at the meekness of Christ and the apparent failure of the cause. All the arguments that we throw now against Judas—hoping that he might force Jesus to take more decisive action and so on—are far more appropriate when applied to Simon.

There may be some significance in the fact that in three out of the four lists of apostles, Simon comes second from the end—immediately before Judas Iscariot. Did the disciples have Simon in mind at the Last Supper when our Lord warned that one of those at the table would betray him? Who more likely than Simon: the one who had been a paid up, card-carrying Zealot? It is possible that the Gospel writers bracketed Simon and Judas because there was always something obviously dangerous about the first and something 'shifty', about the second.

In reality we can make no link between the two. The one was converted and the other was not. He who was so violent by nature and conviction was tamed and calmed by the Son of God. That he went out preaching the good news of the kingdom with the others is undoubted, but he was a most unlikely candidate for conversion. God's little people always are unlikely, because they are not candidates who offer themselves to be chosen, but lost strangers to the grace of God who have been chosen long before the world was founded and called by the Son of God who delights to take unlikely people and use them for his honour.

Thomas—the resolute doubter

'I will not believe it' John 20:25

The English language is peppered with idioms that have been taken from the Bible. There are literally scores of sayings that people use in everyday life, yet they are quite unaware they are quoting Scripture, and many of these are connected with a Bible character: 'Adam's apple', 'Job's comforters', 'Daniel in the lion's den', 'David and Goliath' and, more tragically, 'a Judas'. Similarly, people who are normally quite unfamiliar with the contents of the Bible will find themselves referring to someone as 'a doubting Thomas'. For one single act of determined unbelief, poor Thomas has come down to us in history as a prime example of stubborn refusal to accept anything unless it can be demonstrated by all reasonable means to be true. But does he really deserve that judgement?

There are just eight passages that refer to Thomas in the New Testament. In the first three Gospels and Acts, Thomas's name appears only in the list of apostles: between Bartholomew and Matthew (Matthew 10:3); between Matthew and James (Mark 3:18 and Luke 6:15), and between Philip and Bartholomew (Acts 1:13). It is therefore left to John to introduce him to us in more detail, and the four occasions when he does so are, of course, significant.

We know nothing directly of his parents, his home, or his occupation. These are therefore questions that we must leave to those who prefer to speculate rather than investigate; though since he joined the others in that post-Calvary fishing trip (John 21:1–3), it is very likely he was from the same fishing fraternity. What is certain is that he had a twin brother (or sister) since his name, Thomas, in Aramaic means 'twin', and three times John uses the Greek equivalent (*Didymus*) to describe him, for example: 'Then Thomas (called Didymus) said to the rest …' (11:16). We can only assume that 'Didymus' was chosen as a nickname, since there is no other Thomas in the New Testament that would necessitate an identification to avoid confusion.

Thomas is only known as the doubter—we condemn in others the failures most prevalent in ourselves—but there is more to him than that encounter with the risen Christ. In fact we meet Thomas on three occasions, and each time there is at least a consistency about his character.

Bold and firm resolution

The first occasion we are introduced to the character of Thomas is shortly after the Feast of Dedication late in December AD 29, when the disciples were with Jesus in Jerusalem. Clearly things were beginning to turn dangerous. Jesus had recently spoken of his coming death and some of the Jews were already accusing him of being demon-possessed. Later, in response to a challenge to his identity: 'If you are the Christ, tell us plainly' (John 10:24), our Lord spoke about giving his followers eternal life, and then he identified himself with God: 'My Father, who has given them [my sheep] to me, is greater than all; no one can snatch them out of my Father's hand. I and the Father are one' (v 29–30). That last statement was certainly inflammatory, and many of the Jews prepared to stone him to death. He stayed their hand but reaffirmed his relationship to God which infuriated the Jews even more and they 'tried to seize him, but he escaped their grasp' (10:39).

To make matters worse, no sooner had the apostles retired to the relative security across the Jordan, than a messenger arrived to say that Lazarus, one of the close friends of Jesus, was ill. Bad news was following bad news. The disciples must have been very relieved that for two days Jesus made no move; it would be typical of him to hurry back to Bethany, but not this time. Could he at last see the wisdom of lying low for a while? But no, after two days Jesus invited them: 'Let us go back to Judea' (11:7). One can only assume that there was more than a moment of hesitation among the disciples. It was dangerous to return so soon to Judea—better to let things cool for a while—and there seemed little point hazarding their safety for someone who was only ill. Even Peter was silent! After a long and pregnant pause, they all bubble out their objections: 'But Rabbi, ... a short while ago the Jews tried to stone you, and yet you are going back there?' (v 8). To visit the home of Lazarus meant crossing back into Judea where a pack of wolves would be howling for his blood.

A little parable by Jesus followed to the effect that the work Jesus and his disciples had to do and the time in which they must do it was fixed, and they had nothing to fear. Nothing they could do by way of caution and nothing the enemy could do by way of intrigue, could change the plan of God. Now was the time to go and wake up Lazarus from his sleep. Perhaps most of them missed the point of this parable, because they were eager to grasp a straw and suggest that if Lazarus was only asleep, then he must be past the worst and would soon get well again (v 12); so Jesus spelt out plainly that Lazarus was dead. For the second time he invited the disciples to join him and return to Judea.

It was left to Thomas to stir the party into action: 'Let us also go, that we may die with him' (v 16). Had Thomas grasped what most of the others failed to grasp? Did he realise the meaning of the parable, and did that stiffen his conviction that ultimately they had nothing to lose even if they were to die? The most important thing was to do today's work during the daylight hours.

This was not the bravado of an ignorant man, nor the whim of a fool, it was a serious statement facing grim dangers. All the disciples had been weighing up the risk involved in crossing back into 'enemy territory' and no one was keen to move. Thomas was decided and firm—and rallied the wavering faith of the apostles. He is rarely given the credit he deserves for this; it was a bold and resolute decision, and he meant what he said: 'We will die with him if need be.' This was an act of courage and conviction—incidentally some time before Peter was to make a similar resolution to die with Christ—and it was contagious. Jesus said 'Let's go' and Thomas responded: 'Let's go', and the rest followed. That is not the response of a man without faith.

We can, of course be hypercritical of Thomas and complain that he did not appreciate that Jesus would not end up on the wrong end of rocks, but at the right time on a cross. But that is demanding far too much at this stage. More to the point is to compare our confidence with his. At that moment

Thomas was prepared to take up a 'cross' and follow Christ; of course he would fail to carry through when the crunch finally came and, like all the disciples, he ran away in Gethsemane, but he was as sincere in his determination now as Peter was later (John 13:37). It took courage for Thomas to make the stand that he did on this occasion and to lead the rest in following through. God is pleased with our determination even when we fail to follow through.

Slow spiritual perception

It is not unusual that a day of high spiritual success is followed by a low spiritual failure. We next meet Thomas in John 14. This time, Jesus was not inviting the disciples to accompany him. On the contrary, he was trying to initiate them into living without his physical presence among them. Once again, it was at the time of a Jewish festival. This was the Passover, some four months after the Feast of Dedication, and the whole atmosphere was shot through with tension: the Last Supper, warnings of his impending death, the washing of the disciple's feet, the announcement of betrayal by one of their number, followed by the departure of Judas, a new dimension to the commandment of love and finally a clear and ominous statement: 'My children, I will be with you only a little longer ... Where I am going, you cannot come' (13:33). Peter wanted to know where Jesus was going, and when he was told that he could not follow yet but would later, it was typical of that disciple that he would protest his loyalty and willingness to follow Jesus now. Peter was gently put in his place with a solemn warning that he would soon deny Christ.

Now Jesus spelt out things more clearly for them. His 'going' is not simply to betrayal, trial and death, but to 'My Father's house'. There he would prepare for them to join him and would one day return to take them home. At this point he could assume that they would understand all this: 'You know the way to the place where I am going' (14:4). They were well-instructed Jews and had been with Jesus for three years; much of his teaching had revolved around parables and illustrations of heaven and they should understand by now how anyone becomes a member of that kingdom. After all, they had each been out preaching about the kingdom and the way into it.

Thomas now revealed how tragically slow he had been to grasp the elements of the message of Jesus; whether or not he spoke on behalf of all the disciples, we cannot know, but since he was the only one to respond, it clearly revealed his own mind at least. Thomas was blunt—he neither understood the where nor the how of Jesus' statements, and he said so: 'Lord, we don't know where you are going, so how can we know the way' (v 5). That, of course, was a perfectly logical sequence. If a man does not know what his destination is, he cannot possibly know the route!

For three years Thomas had lived and worked with Christ and still he did not understand the reality of heaven and how to get there! Thomas was a very down to earth man: if he believed in something, he would give his life for it—but he had to be convinced of it first. Heaven did not rate highly in his thinking; eternal and spiritual issues were placed distinctly second to 'the cause'. Three years with Christ, and he still did not know 'the way'. To respond to their Lord's statement and promise in vs 2–3 with the counter: 'We don't know where you are going' was crass spiritual blindness to an enormous degree. Even the Pharisees understood the claim when Jesus spoke of 'my Father'. This was because, in reality Thomas did not know Christ—and that is precisely what Christ claimed: 'If you really knew me, you would know my Father as well' (v 7). At least his objection drew from Christ the magnificent claim: 'I am the way and the truth and the life. No one comes to the Father except through me' (v 6).

Obstinate unbelief

We do not know where Thomas was when all the other disciples were together on that evening of the first day of the week when Jesus appeared among them (John 20:19–24). One suspects he should have been there, because Jesus had planned this as the occasion when he would send the Holy Spirit among them (v 22), commission them with the authority of the gospel (v 23), and give them a vital Bible study (Luke 24:36–49). At least he had courage to be elsewhere, when the rest had locked themselves in 'for fear of the Jews' (John 20:19)—or else he was despondently without hope! But when the ten apostles excitedly told him of their experience with the risen Christ, Thomas obstinately refused to believe.

In the first place Thomas disputed their testimony. They must surely have been changed men, yet by refusing to believe them, he was accusing them of either deliberate deceit or foolish imagination; neither of which was likely under the circumstances. Thomas could be forgiven had he been sad, glad and hopeful over the next week: sad at missing out the first time, glad for the rest of the group and what it all meant, and hopeful that his turn would soon come. But none of this was the case. He was not even resentful. Thomas was just totally unbelieving or at best very sceptical. But it was not only the testimony of these ten that Thomas disputed. Some of the women had burst in excitedly with news of the risen Christ (John 20:18)—and Thomas was present then (Luke 24:9). Shortly after, Peter and John testified to seeing the empty tomb (John 20:3–9). Thomas may or may not have been there when the two disciples from Emmaus arrived with the news of their conversation with Christ on the road out of Jerusalem; Luke 24:33 refers to the 'eleven' but that could be just a handle for the apostles rather like the 'Twelve', or else we must suppose a gap in time between verses 35 and 36 during which Thomas had left. Surely all this evidence made the story of the ten apostles at least credible.

But more than all this, Thomas insisted upon his own conditions for belief. He was prepared to believe in a resurrection, but he must see and touch, or else there would be no possibility of his believing. Thomas appears, not unnaturally, to be emotionally het-up at this point. The word translated 'put' is a little softer than the one Thomas used. His word is drawn from the verb to cast or throw; it seems that he wanted to 'push' his finger and hand into the nail prints and the spear wound.

Rationalism is an age old superstition that demands 'empirical proof' before belief is possible; the eighteenth century Scottish philosopher, David Hume, set off millions in the wrong direction when he demanded that unless a thing can be reasoned and examined in experience, then it cannot be believed; as a result, Hume denied all miracles and the supernatural. Thomas was a forerunner of rationalism and he is set as a warning to us all. He would later learn that God's definition of faith is substantial confidence in the unseen and the untested: 'being sure of what we hope for and certain of what we do not see' (Hebrews 11:1). Down the centuries since that statement of unbelief by Thomas, millions have unwittingly aped him: 'Unless I can see, I will not believe.' Whilst on this occasion, the Lord pandered to his obstinacy, he rarely does; in fact his promise is that there is greater happiness for those who trust without physical sight (v 29). Doubtless Thomas lived to regret his persistent and stubborn unbelief.

Another tragedy in this story is that Thomas continued in his unbelief for a whole week. What a drag on the conversations of the other ten he must have been! Whenever they talked about their experience, Thomas would persist in 'Unless ... I will not'. He was a loyal but despondent disciple. Paul later referred to a man like this as one who is 'to be pitied more than all men' (1 Corinthians 15:19). For a professing disciple of Christ to doubt the reality of the resurrection is the greatest of tragedies.

For a whole week Christ left Thomas to his own miserable confusion. He does not always provide the answers that we want within the time-scale that we demand. Interestingly, when our Lord at last appeared to Thomas, the circumstances were remarkably similar to the previous week: the same house, the same locked doors, the same company, the same standing among them and the same greeting; perhaps the only difference was the presence of Thomas. And Jesus turned his attention directly to this wide-eyed unbeliever. All eyes were upon him, but the most hurtful were those of Christ himself. For every demand of Thomas, there was a command of Christ: 'Put your finger here; see my hands. Reach out your hand, and put it into my side. Stop doubting and believe' (v 27).

This was not the first time Jesus had invited his disciples to 'Touch me and see' (Luke 24:39) and on that occasion it is doubtful whether they took up the invitation. Now Thomas was overwhelmed by the fact that not only was he standing before the risen Christ, but that Christ knew precisely the words that Thomas had used as a condition of his believing. The Lord was virtually quoting Thomas back to himself.

Overwhelmed by the risen Christ

We would, of course, expect this, but the response of Thomas to the invitation of Christ was simple and powerful. We still do not know, in spite of paintings that show him placing his hand into our Lord's side, whether he ever took up Christ's invitation; I am as equally certain that he did not as some commentators are certain that he did! However, his response was to cry out an acknowledgement of total confidence and commitment: 'My

Lord and my God' (John 20:28). This was a massive claim. Contrary to the foolish imagination of the Watchtower Movement, Thomas did not look to Christ and declare 'My Lord' and then glance towards heaven and acknowledge 'My God'! Both titles were offered to Christ. He who was a convinced sceptic now became the most certain of them all. None of the other disciples had yet declared so positively their belief in the deity of Christ; Thomas was now as convinced a believer as he had been a confirmed doubter.

What followed was a gentle rebuke to Thomas and a great encouragement to centuries of Christians that would follow: 'Because you have seen me, you have believed; blessed are those who have not seen and yet have believed' (v 29). Jesus drew a significant lesson from Thomas that there is greater joy in walking with Christ by faith than by sight. This was something Peter urged upon the young Christians who would shortly go through the fires of persecution in their new-found love for Christ: 'Though you have not seen him, you love him; and even though you do not see him now, you believe in him and are filled with an inexpressible and glorious joy, for you are receiving the goal of your faith, the salvation of your souls' (1 Peter 1:8–9). It is the same failure of Thomas that leads many, even Christians, to demand signs and wonders as a bolster to their faith. The test in these hard days in Western society, when few are coming to a living faith and many are losing what faith they had, is whether we are prepared to go on living in the light of the promises of Christ even though we see little evidence around us of his presence.

In writing his Gospel record, with this story John has come full circle. At the beginning he declared that 'The Word was God' (1:1), and his purpose in the Gospel was that the readers would come to believe that 'Jesus is the Christ, the Son of God' (20:31); here is the first disciple to make that open claim: 'My Lord and my God.' The verse with which John signs off this whole episode is significant. There were many other miracles and signs that Jesus did, and his disciples saw them all; slowly and reluctantly they came to understand the meaning, and Thomas stands as a warning and example to all who follow. The evidence is before us, and all who read must decide for or against Christ on the basis of that evidence; nothing more certain will ever be available.

The Thomas of legend

It may be unfortunately appropriate, that even today Thomas is the cause of more vigorous debate than any of the other apostles on account of certain ancient texts that claim to originate from his pen. The first is the *Acts of Thomas*—the earliest copy of which is dated in the 10th century AD, though it is thought the original may have been produced in the first half of the third century. This is the story in brief: After the ascension of Christ, the apostles gathered together and portioned out the areas of the world that each would evangelise. Thomas was given India but, true to character, he begged to be excused because of 'weakness of the flesh' and adamantly refused to go. Christ miraculously intervened and Thomas became a servant to an Indian king who ruled in the region of Afghanistan, Punjab and Sind. After various events and miracles, the king, whose name was Gundafar, was converted and a church was formed. The legend has it that Thomas was speared to death in India in AD 72.

The second ancient text is the *Revelation of Thomas*—virtually unknown until 1908—which professes to be a revelation to Thomas of the end of the world. There are just two copies existing, both dating from the fifth century. Of more interest, but of no better history, is the *Infancy Gospel of Thomas*, possibly written as early as the mid second century and, as the name suggests, it fills in the gaps of those silent twelve years of our Lord's childhood. Irenaus, a Christian leader, referred to it around AD 185 and condemned it as heretical; our earliest copy comes from the sixth century, and it contains many fanciful stories, such as Jesus making birds of clay which then fly away, and more grotesque accounts of him killing playmates—and others—who displeased him. When God is silent, men have never been slow to fill the gaps with their wild imaginations.

Finally, and of more significance, is the *Gospel of Thomas*, the existence of which had been known since the fourth century, but no copy was available until one (buried in the fifth century) was discovered in 1945 in Upper Egypt as part of the Nag Hammadi Library. In this false gospel there is no virgin birth, no crucifixion, no atonement, no healing miracles, and Thomas is the twin brother of Jesus; it claims to reveal the 'secret sayings' of Jesus. According to a recent best-seller *The Da Vinci Code*—a book of fiction dressed in a thin and ragged garb of 'scholarship'—this reveals the true story of Christ which was suppressed by the early church. This is not the place to debate ancient false writings, but it is certainly amazing how much has been attributed to an apostle who is mentioned, apart from the listings, only on three occasions and each in the Gospel of John. Thomas is supposedly the patron saint of carpenters, builders and many other trades; his relics are still venerated in Edessa, and 'St Thomas's Sunday' is always one week after Easter!

Whilst the fingers of generations of Christians have pointed accusingly at Thomas for his doubting, he is there in Scripture simply because he is so much like all of us. The most resolute and bold may doubt, just as the most loyal and faithful may doubt. But in the story of Thomas the Lord was determined to settle the issue for all time. He will not always pander to our demands for 'reasonable evidence', but the testimony of two millenniums of Christian thinkers, martyrs, missionaries and teachers testifies to the reality of Christ's resurrection. Without a firm belief in the literal, historical resurrection of Christ, and a resulting conviction that he is 'Lord and God', no one can have life in his name. Thomas was thoughtful but courageous when he had made up his mind, mystified yet devoted to his Lord, unbelieving but tenacious when he was convinced, hopeless at the cross yet when he met with the risen Christ his words scaled higher than any of the other disciples. Resolute doubter he may have been, but resolute in faith also.

James—the son of Alphaeus, and Judas Thaddaeus—the son of James

W e know little about this son of Alphaeus, and even less about his father! However, Matthew was also a son of Alphaeus (Mark 2:14) and it is possible, though by no means certain, that Matthew and James were brothers. The uncertainty lies in the fact that the two brothers James and John are always linked together as a pair in the lists of apostles in Matthew 10:3, Mark 3:18, Luke 6:15 and Acts 1:13, whereas Matthew and James are never so linked. However, Mark and Luke (in Acts 1:13) both separate Peter and Andrew and make no family connection between them. Matthew and James are placed alongside each other only in Acts 1, but even then there is no hint of a relationship: James is referred to as 'James son of Alphaeus', yet Luke gives no clue that Matthew is of the same family. This uncertainty means that it would be unwise for us to make anything of this possible relationship.

James is frequently identified with 'James the younger (or the little or less)' who is referred to in Mark 15:40 as the son of one of the women named Mary who stood watching from a distance as the terrible events unfolded at Calvary. However, Mark gives him a brother named Joses (Joseph in Matthew 27:56) and it is remarkable that his more well known brother Matthew (if they were brothers) should not have been mentioned. On the other hand, the Gospel writers were often quite loose in the way they identified their characters; only seven verses later, Mark drops James altogether and refers simply to 'Mary the mother of Joses', and in the very next verse (Mark 16:1) she is 'Mary the mother of James'! Even more confusing is the fact that if this is the Mary referred to in John 19:25, then she was the wife of Clopas and not Alphaeus—unless, of course, Alphaeus had died and Mary had remarried, or this is a different James from the apostle. Unfortunately there is far too much supposition in all this for us to build a character study upon it. Besides, even if all this conjecture could be proved, it would not teach us a great deal, except that James enjoyed the privilege of a godly mother and possibly a godly father also.

The *Catholic Encyclopedia* identifies 'James the Less' with James the brother of Jesus, and many of the early legends that follow him make the same error by confusing the two. From a Roman Catholic perspective it has the sole merit of distancing the 'brother of our Lord' from a blood tie with Christ—since they believe his 'brothers' of Matthew 13:55 are half brothers from a different mother—and thus bolstering the fragile doctrine of the perpetual virginity of Mary the mother of Jesus.

However, if we know nothing of James the apostle beyond his name in the lists, even that silence is instructive, for we are considering one of the apostles here. James the son of Alphaeus was at some point called by Christ to be one of the Twelve. He stayed close to Christ for the entire three years of the Lord's public ministry, was sent out on the preaching tours along with the others, and came back with the same glowing stories of success. He listened to, prayed with and watched carefully all that Jesus taught and did. He grew in his muddled understanding as slowly as the others, doubted as they did and came to a painfully sluggish belief just as they all did. And finally, when convinced of Christ's resurrection, James the son of Alphaeus became one of the leaders in the church at Jerusalem, participated in the decisions and advice that was sent out to the infant churches, took his share of preaching to fulfil the great commission, and finally, though just how we do not know, died, probably a martyr's death. Yet for all this, we know nothing specifically about him that does not belong to them all.

We would expect it to be otherwise, and this is why some have desperately tried to link him with anyone in the biblical records that would expand our knowledge of him; but God, in his wisdom, has kept the details a secret so that we might learn that, across two thousand years of the story of the church, so much has been achieved for the sake of the gospel by the little people who, though well known in their day, have slipped from this world with barely a visible legacy to record. Yet in reality, they have done so much to fulfil the Master's plan for the kingdom of God.

Judas Thaddaeus—the son of James

The identification of Thaddaeus can be only a little more certain. This is the name used by Matthew and Mark in their Gospels, whilst Luke, both in his Gospel and in Acts, refers to him as 'Judas son of James'. Literally the Greek here is 'Judas of James' and that caused the *Authorised Version* to conjecture 'Judas the brother of James' but that is very unlikely; when the genitive alone is used then convention would demand that we read it as 'son of', and if the brother is intended then normally the word 'brother' (*adelphos*) is inserted, as for example in Mark 5:37 and 6:3.

To confuse the picture a little, some Greek texts in Matthew 10:3 and Mark 3:18 read 'Lebbaeus' instead, and thus the *Authorised Version* and the *New King James Version* have: 'Lebbaeus, whose surname was Thaddaeus'. Even the meaning of this name 'Lebbaeus' has given rise to a debate of which there is no immediate conclusion—we just do not know. Few churches have been named after him and Thaddaeus never became a popular Christian name, unlike all the other apostles. Legend dismissed him as being sent to Armenia, Syria and Persia where he was finally killed, shot through by archers—though there are alternatives. He has variously been identified with Thomas and even regarded as the twin brother of Jesus!

We cannot even be sure which James he was the son of. It is not impossible that he was the son of the apostle James, son of Alphaeus. However this is very unlikely, since he is never linked with that James in the lists of apostles, and we would have expected Matthew and Mark to have made this obvious connection, but they do not even inform us that he was the 'son of James'.

Often 'Judas son of James' is thought to be the author of the New Testament letter under the name of Jude. This is because Jude 1 opens with the claim: 'Jude, a servant of Jesus Christ and a brother of James'. This, of course, influenced the translation referred to above in some versions at Luke 6:15 and Acts 1:13. However, the James of Jude 1 was most likely the brother of the Lord who became a leading elder in the Jerusalem church (Acts 15:13; 21:18). He certainly cannot have been the brother of the apostle James who was martyred by Herod as early as Acts 12. Besides, if the author of the letter was the apostle Judas, it would have been more natural to introduce himself with that word 'apostle', as both Paul and

Peter do, rather than only the word 'servant'; also, he would have no need to rely upon the authority of his 'brother' James. In fact, the author of the letter appears to clearly distinguish himself from the apostles (see Jude v 17). So, Judas Thaddaeus, the apostle, is not to be confused with this brother of Jesus (Matthew 13:55) who wrote the New Testament letter.

Besides the betrayer, there are four other men with the name of Judas in the New Testament, and perhaps that is fortunate because it rescues a name that would otherwise have been avoided in later history. One is a brother of Jesus (Matthew 13:55) who later left us the New Testament letter under his name. A second Judas is referred to by Gamaliel in Acts 5:37—a Galilean who stirred up trouble and was dealt with by the Romans and his followers were scattered. A third was a Jew with whom Paul lodged whilst he was in Damascus, and the fourth was sent by the church at Jerusalem to Antioch along with Paul, Barnabas and Silas to relay the decision of the Jerusalem conference to the churches (Acts 15:22); evidently, perhaps for obvious reasons, he preferred to be known as Barsabbas.

Once we leave uncertainty behind us, there are only two certain facts left with regard to this Judas Thaddaeus, son of James. In the first place, he was an apostle. And all that has been said of James of Alphaeus must be true also of Judas Thaddaeus. There is significance in the fact that here is an apostle of whom we know so little. Even the legends are unusually hesitant in imagining his future course. We have his names, presumably alternatives reflect the preference not to use the name Judas after the betrayal, and little more.

But there is one more fact available to us that introduces something of his character. During the final supper with the Twelve, Jesus began to prepare them for his departure. It was a very intimate and personal discourse, full of instruction and encouragement. In order to settle their minds, Jesus promised that he would send the Holy Spirit to them and that he, the Spirit, would make real to them the presence of Christ among them. In fact, he promised that whilst the world would no longer see him, 'you will see me' (John 14:19), and to those who love him and are loved by the Father 'I too will love him and show myself to him (v 21). The word 'show' is translated as 'manifest' in some versions because it refers to something laid open for all to see; the word *emphanizo* was originally used of an official report or open document.

This was all too much for Judas Thaddaeus, and presumably for the others as well, who could not conceive how Jesus would make himself known to his disciples in such a way that the world would not be able to see him as well. And he said so: 'But, Lord, why do you intend to show yourself to us and not to the world?' (John 14:22). Just sixteen words in English, thirteen in the Greek—and that is the total of all his recorded words in history. Perhaps a more literal translation of what Judas Thaddaeus really said will help to bring out the exclamation of surprise: ' Lord, what can it be: that you are about to reveal yourself to us, and not to all the world?'

This is the only occasion when John refers to this apostle, and he is careful to distinguish him from his notorious namesake: 'Judas, (not Judas Iscariot) ...', but there is some similarity with what must have been in the betrayer's mind at this time. Judas Thaddaeus could not understand how the kingdom of God could possibly come unless the whole world could see it. Surely, if the Messiah is to make a public disclosure of his power and glory, for that is the implication of the verb *emphanizo*, then it would only vindicate his name and his kingdom if everyone could see him.

This, of course, revealed the lack of spiritual perception on the part of Judas Thaddaeus. The kingdom that Jesus would leave behind was secret, as so many of his parables had been teaching them if only they had had minds to understand—the yeast and mustard seed for example. Until his final return at the end of time, the kingdom of God would always remain secret and hidden in the hearts and lives of all who believe in him. Jesus went on to teach Judas Thaddaeus, and the rest, of the value of the Holy Spirit and the importance of understanding the kingdom in terms of the Spirit and not the world (vs 23–31). The kingdom of God is when the Father and Son come and 'make our home' with those who love him and obey his teaching. There is, of course, a final revelation of the kingdom, but that will not be until the end of time when the Son of God returns in his glory; this is the meaning of his 'not yet' parables such as that of the nobleman from a distant country (Luke 19:11).

Too frequently in its long history, the church has become impatient with the quiet and often secret work of the Spirit, and has tried to establish the kingdom of God with the sword. The disciples tried the same in the garden and learnt the bitter lesson that this in not the way. The true kingdom of God is seen in the quality lives of men and women indwelt by the Holy Spirit; this is what changed the course of history over the first three centuries after Pentecost. It is certainly not seen in 'Christendom' extending its borders by military force, or even by churches trying to 'Christianise' society by some form of Christian socialism. This is not to say that governments should not be reminded of biblical standards for a healthy society, but that must never be confused with the kingdom of God.

Paul later grappled with the same problem of explaining spiritual realities to those who had little spiritual understanding, in fact he concluded that it was impossible: 'This is what we speak, not in words taught us by human wisdom but in words taught by the Spirit, expressing spiritual truths in spiritual words. The man without the Spirit does not accept the things that come from the Spirit of God, for they are foolishness to him, and he cannot understand them, because they are spiritually discerned' (1 Corinthians 2:13–14). That is a sad comment on the apostles at this particular moment. But it is precisely what Jesus had taught to Nicodemus at the beginning of his ministry: 'I tell you the truth, no one can see the kingdom of God unless he is born again (John 3:3).

When, later, the Lord went on to talk of the world hating those who follow Christ, because 'it hated me first' (15:18), he was teaching the same thing. One reason why all across the world today Christians are hated and persecuted by atheism, Hinduism, Buddhism and Islam is simply because those religions cannot understand that the kingdom of God is intended as no threat to their governments; but because it is secret and hidden—in the lives of its followers—that very fact appears to be a threat.

Judas Thaddaeus revealed the poor thinking of too many, both within and outside the church, in every age of post Pentecost history. To the human mind, power and glory is only understood in terms of armies and empires. But the true manifestation of the glory of Christ is seen in every individual within whom the Father and Son take up residence by the person of the Holy Spirit. That is what it means to know Christ. Sadly, by John 16:17–18 the apostles had still not understood what Jesus was teaching them: 'What does he mean by saying "In a little while you will see me no more, and then after a little while you will see me ..." We don't understand what he is saying.' The sixteen words of Judas Thaddaeus are the sad legacy of his recorded life, but they are left as a warning to the church against an earthly and worldly view of the glory of Christ.

Judas Iscariot—apostasy from privilege

'Woe to that man who betrays the Son of Man! It would be better for him if he had not been born' Matthew 26:24

The story of Judas as Peter might have told it

He was with us right from the beginning. Jesus chose him to be a disciple when he called the other eleven of us. He seemed to be quite attentive when Jesus was talking to us; in fact he was very enthusiastic about the whole idea of being a disciple of Christ. He used to talk about the great things that would happen in the future if we all stood by Christ. He was especially keen for Jesus to talk about the kingdom.

We never learnt very much about his background. He was about the same age as the rest of us and his father was called Simon, though he was no relative of mine! His name Judas is a form of Judah, and it means 'praise'—pity he had such an inappropriate name! We called him Iscariot because he came from a place called Kerioth-Hezron in Judah, about twelve miles south of Hebron.

One day Jesus asked him if he would look after our money bag and act as our treasurer. We never had much money, but we pooled what we had, and from time to time people would encourage us by giving towards our support. We were never quite sure why Jesus chose Judas to look after the money, Matthew seemed the natural choice to most of us because of his background in finance. Sometimes there were discussions about why we were so low on cash when we knew that we had been given some money recently, but we never suspected that Judas was pilfering our small income. Looking back I can see that although he was with us right from the start, he was never really one of us, There was always something different about him; something cold and remote. Before Jesus was arrested in Gethsemane, there were three things that should have alerted us to the kind of man he was.

I remember one day when we were at Capernaum; a crowd had been following Jesus until he said some pretty hard things to them about what it would cost if they threw in their lot with us, and that soon thinned out the followers. Then Jesus turned and asked us if we would leave him as well. Of course, I protested that there was no one else to whom we could go because only he had the words of eternal life. Then Jesus said something very odd: 'Did I not choose you, the Twelve, and one of you is a devil?' Sometime later when he rounded on me and accused me of doing the devil's work for him, I linked these two and thought he must have been talking about me. That really cut me up I can tell you. But at that time when Jesus said 'one of you is a devil' it set us thinking for a bit; but life was hectic in those days and we soon forgot it. We certainly never thought of Judas; after all, when we went out preaching and healing, Judas came and did as well as any of us. We went out in pairs, but I can't remember who he was twinned with. I think it might have been Simon the convert from the Zealot party, and if so, it's quite clear that Jesus was testing out Simon's loyalty, because if ever two men could have teamed up for betrayal when the wind was blowing against us, it would have been those two. Fortunately Simon the Zealot stood firm, but even he never got the measure of two-faced Judas.

Then, on another occasion, just a week before the Passover, we were having a meal at the house of Lazarus in Bethany—a wonderfully hospitable family they were, and even more so after the incredible miracle on Lazarus! Mary, the sister of Lazarus and Martha, took some special oil and began to pour it all over Jesus. From the sweet smell that filled the whole house, even we men knew that this was a particularly expensive perfume—we reckoned it was worth about three hundred denarii. I have to admit that it looked a waste and we all thought the same, but it was Judas who said so. I can remember his words even now, and the harsh voice and stony face that accompanied them: 'Why wasn't this perfume sold and the money given to the poor? It was worth a year's wages!' There was a stunned silence for a moment and I think Mary began to cry. Then Jesus came to her defence and we all felt guilty. Judas just turned away in disgust.

Although we didn't know it at the time of course, this was the last straw for Judas, and shortly after this episode he went to the chief priests and offered to lead them to our secret rendezvous for thirty pieces of silver—so much for his concern for the poor! Thirty pieces of silver was equivalent to about one hundred and twenty denarii, that's a little less than half a year's wages for a labourer; or to put it another way, according to Moses in the Law, it was the price paid in compensation if your bull injured someone's slave.

The next occasion was at the special Passover meal we had together—the last supper we ever had with Jesus. All twelve of us were there with him, and we had a feeling that everything was not well. Jesus seemed more sad and quiet than usual; he obviously had a lot on his mind—and we now know what that was, but we didn't at the time. He talked to us about the future, but we were so dull then that we didn't grasp the true significance of a lot that he was saying. Then he said something that made us all sit up and take notice: 'I am not referring to all of you; I know those I have chosen. But this is to fulfil the Scripture: "He who shares my bread has lifted up his heel against me." I am telling you now before it happens, so that when it does happen you will believe that I am He.'

We didn't really understand this, so he added 'One of you will betray me.' Everyone started talking at once, and I whispered to John—who was sitting opposite me and next to Jesus—to ask him who he was talking about. Jesus replied that it would be the one to whom he gave a piece of bread when he had dipped it in the bowl. Then he gave it to Judas, and I heard Judas say 'Is it me, Lord?' Then Jesus replied quietly and solemnly 'You have said so.' Still Judas sat there and gradually the others stopped talking. Jesus looked up, and staring at Judas said firmly: 'What you are going to do, do quickly.' None of the others knew what this meant, and they thought that Jesus was sending Judas out to but some more food for the meal, or maybe to give something to the poor, since he had earlier expressed such a concern for them. John and I said nothing. Everything in me wanted to get up and use my little sword there and then, but I couldn't move; anyway, even I did not quite follow what it was all about. It was impossible to imagine any one of us turning Jesus over to his enemies.

Judas got up, opened the door, and disappeared into the night. We heard him running downstairs and out into the street. A door slammed and everything was silent. It was as black as olives out there. That was the last time we got a good look at Judas. Later in the evening Jesus referred to him as 'the one doomed to destruction'. Judas had left before the end of the meal and was not there when Jesus broke the bread and handed round the wine as symbols of his coming death.

You know the rest of the story. Jesus did a lot more talking and then we went out to the Mount of Olives where he prayed for a long time; he was clearly suffering a great deal and I'm afraid we were no help to him—we were so exhausted that we fell asleep just when he needed us most. Then we crossed the Kidron Valley and came to the olive grove that we called Gethsemane. We hadn't been there long before a detachment of soldiers arrived on the scene together with officials from the chief priests and Pharisees. At first we couldn't understand how they discovered us here; this was a private place and it was our secret rendezvous. Then a figure broke from the group and came towards Jesus, and it all became clear. I saw him come up to Jesus and embrace him and kiss him on the cheek. But it was not until he said 'Hail, Master' that I realised who it was. I can still hear the reply Jesus gave him, it was so quiet and as if he was appealing just one more time to Judas: 'Friend, why are you here? Judas, would you betray the Son of Man with a kiss?'

I'm afraid I lost my temper at that and lunged out with my sword. On reflection it was a stupid thing to do because we were heavily outnumbered, but at that moment there was no time to reflect; typically of me, I just acted and let my mind catch up later. But when it was obvious that Jesus had no intention of resisting arrest, I lost my nerve and ran away with all the others. We learnt that Judas had later gone to the temple and had thrown the money down and went out and hanged himself. Apparently, John had contacts in the palace of the high priest so we knew what went on, Judas said, 'I have sinned, for I have betrayed innocent blood.' But he had earned his money and the priests were not interested in him any more: 'What is that to us?' they replied. 'That is your responsibility.' That's when he went out and hanged himself ; and a pretty gruesome affair it was by all accounts. His body broke from the noose and when it crashed to the ground … well, Luke tells you the rest in his account of the early church.

Looking back, he was never really one of us. He stole money from our account and was always a bit shifty. Now I think about it, whenever he addressed Jesus, it was never 'Lord', but only 'Rabbi'. It is obvious now that Judas always had a very different idea from that of the Lord himself of why Jesus was here and what he meant by 'the kingdom'.

We know very little more about Judas than our recollection by Peter above. One writer comments: 'He swore fealty to the banner of Jesus with youthful enthusiasm, though with an unbroken will' (Krummacher) and from a human point of view that is correct. His life stands as a tragic monument to apostasy from privilege. Unlike any of the other apostles, writers have clashed in direct contradiction to one another in assessing the true character of Judas: they range from those who attribute to him only good, though misguided, motives, to those who see Judas as the devil incarnate. In reality he was not all bad, few men are. But he gave way to his evil tendencies and over time his whole life was absorbed by Satan until he lost control of his decisions and became a tool in the hand of a higher and more malevolent power. The very fact that he was not the devil incarnate makes his story a more serious warning on the danger of apostasy from privilege.

The privileges of Judas

There can be no doubt that Judas knew the message of salvation—he had been one of the Twelve for three years. He heard the message, saw the miracles, listened to the teaching and watched the life of Jesus of Nazareth, but at no point did he see in him more than 'Rabbi'. Judas stood by and heard Jesus warn: 'From within, out of men's hearts, come evil thoughts, sexual immorality, theft, murder, adultery, greed, malice, deceit, lewdness, envy, slander, arrogance and folly. All these evils come from inside and make a man unclean' (Mark 7:21–22). At least some in that list must have struck close to the heart of Judas. More than this, Judas had engaged in service for Jesus. Acts 1:25 refers to his 'apostolic ministry'. He was made the treasurer of the Twelve, went out on the evangelistic mission to proclaim the kingdom of God , and came back with the same excited report along with the rest. But, like Demas, he was a man with the gospel in his mouth but the world in his heart (2 Timothy 4:10).

Deep involvement in activity for the name of Christ is no guarantee of a true understanding of the gospel or a true relationship with Christ himself; it can all too easily be a self deceiving blind. Jesus made this very clear in words that ought to have made Judas think carefully: 'Not everyone who says to me, "Lord, Lord," will enter the kingdom of heaven, but only he who does the will of my Father who is in heaven. Many will say to me on that day, "Lord, Lord, did we not prophesy in your name, and in your name drive out demons and perform many miracles?" Then I will tell them plainly, "I never knew you. Away from me, you evildoers!'"(Matthew 7:21–23). Luke seems to hint at this when he adds meaningfully: 'Judas, called Iscariot, *one of the Twelve*' (Luke 22:3, 47). To be an apostle did not make him a true disciple.

But it was not as though Judas had no opportunity to repent. Judas was present when Jesus shared the fact that not all the Twelve were of the same mind: 'There are some of you who do not believe …Have I not chosen you, the Twelve? Yet one of you is a devil!' (John 6:64,70). Later, he was sitting close to Jesus at the final meal when the Lord having washed the feet of his disciples warned: 'I know those I have chosen. But this is to fulfil the scripture: 'He who shares my bread has lifted up his heel against me. I tell you the truth, one of you is going to betray me. The Son of Man will go just as it is written about him. But woe to that man who betrays the Son of Man! It would be better for him if he had not been born' (John 13:18, 21 and Matthew 26:24). The full text of Psalm 41:9 to which Jesus was referring, would doubtless have been known to Judas: 'Even my close friend, whom I trusted, he who shared my bread, has lifted up his heel against me.' Judas heard in his mind the words 'close friend … trusted … shared my bread … against me' and still he could harden his heart.

In fact, on that very occasion when Judas looked across the table and queried: 'Surely not I, Rabbi?', the reply from Jesus could not have been more clear 'Yes, it is you.' That can only have been an appeal to his conscience even at this late stage, since he already had the thirty pieces of silver jingling in his pocket. But there was one last rapier thrust designed to pierce his mind and bring him to repentance: 'What you are about to do, do quickly' (John 13:27). There was still time to throw his ill-gotten money back, he knew what he was doing, and he knew that the Master knew also—that fact alone was evidence that he was far more than a mere 'Rabbi'. But a man may resist the conviction of the Holy Spirit until he is too hardened to return—as Hebrews 6:4–6 and 10:26–27 frighteningly remind us.

The apostasy of Judas

There have been long debates over the reasons why Judas finally betrayed Christ: Was he disillusioned with the progress of the kingdom? Did he always have an agenda that would never fit the purposes of Christ? Was he motivated by nothing more profound than simple greed—stealing from the purse and gaining a few shekels of silver for the betrayal? Or did Judas never imagine that Christ would allow himself to be taken, and hoped that the betrayal would precipitate the establishing of Christ's kingdom by forcing his hand?

Whatever his reasons, two things are clear: Judas had no love for Christ, and no understanding of who he really was. His spiritual eyes were blind, and religious privilege without affection for Christ is worse than of no value. Judas could never see things in a spiritual light, and the worship that Mary showed was nothing better than wasteful extravagance to him (John 12:3–6). But his final fall was no sudden reverse of an otherwise blameless character. In recording his treachery, John is careful to note that he 'used to' help himself to what was in the common purse (v 6); the tense of the verb is deliberate: he did it often. What sort of man could pilfer from Jesus—again and again? At some time during those three years, Judas, in mind though not in body, joined the many disciples who 'turned back and no longer followed him' (John 6:66). Perhaps it was on that very occasion when Jesus had challenged the Twelve: 'You do not want to leave me too, do you?' (v 67), because he went on to warn them, 'Have I not chosen you, the Twelve? Yet one of you is a devil!' (v 70). Peter thought he spoke for all the apostles when he declared 'Lord, to whom shall we go? You have the words of eternal life. We believe and know that you are the Holy One of God' (vs 68–69), but there was one among them who believed none of that and was looking elsewhere for life.

It is deeply significant that when Jesus warned that one of the Twelve would betray him, each of the disciples questioned 'Surely not I, *Lord*?', whereas when the spotlight swung round to Judas his response was 'Surely not I, *Rabbi*?' (Matthew 26:22,25). Never once is he recorded as referring to Christ as Lord. That he was a great teacher could hardly be denied, but to use the word 'Lord' (*kurios*) implied an authority and superiority that Judas was clearly unwilling to acknowledge. That made it all the easier for him to betray Christ; it is easy to turn away from him when we do not appreciate who he is. At the point of betrayal his voice mocked Christ with the words: 'Greetings, Rabbi' (Matthew 26:49). It was a bold, brash kiss that finally identified Christ—an act of love from a heart of stone.

Only too tragically the real motivator behind Judas is plainly revealed to us: 'One of you is a devil ... Satan entered Judas ... the devil had already prompted Judas... to betray Jesus' (John 6:70; Luke 22:3; John 13:2). But neither this, nor the fact that his betrayal was both planned by God and prophesied in the Scriptures, could detract from his personal responsibility. When John records 'the devil had already prompted Judas Iscariot ... to betray Jesus', he intends to inform us that this plan had been long in the development in his mind. The prompting to evil may come from the devil, but the decision is ours. This must always be remembered by those who consider that Judas was somehow treated unfairly by God. Of course it was God's plan for Christ to be betrayed in this way, and of course the psalmist David foretold the detail on more than one occasion (Psalm 41:9; 69:25; 109:8—compare Acts 1:20) as did Zechariah (11:12–13), but it was Judas whose heart was hard and who decided against his conscience.

Apart from these dreadful comments that Judas was motivated, even driven, by Satan, we may partly understand him as a man who just could not believe. After all, even the Lord's own brothers refused to accept Jesus as anything more than an enthusiast until they were confronted by him after his resurrection (Mark 3:21 and John 7:3–4). But there was something more final and ingrained about Judas. When Jesus referred to Judas in his prayer to the Father, he called him the 'son of destruction' (John 17:12 *English Standard Version*). The NIV 'the one doomed to destruction' has tried to bring out the connection of the Greek that is not clear in a literal translation. The phrase 'son of' implies that it was his very nature to be lost. Someone has called his apostasy 'the natural gravitation of his character'. Exactly the same expression is found in 2 Thessalonians 2:3 where the man of lawlessness is referred to as 'the son of destruction' (ESV)

His was a terrible end. Just why the enormity of his crime broke in on Judas when it did, is another mystery in the character of this evil man, but that which once tempted him now tormented him. When he returned to the temple with the silver and tried to return it, admitting for the first time and too late: 'I have sinned, for I have betrayed innocent blood', he was met with a blank stare and a haughty indifference. The priests had their prize and Judas had his, and as far as they were concerned that was the end of the story: 'What is that to us. That is your responsibility.'

That last phrase was just two words from the lips of the priest which we can only translate as 'You see to it'. And Judas did! Throwing down the silver in disgust at himself he went out and hanged himself, and apparently his body fell from the rope and split open on the rocks. For their part the priests were left with an embarrassing decision. As they gathered up the silver they realised it was 'blood money'—in more ways than they would admit—and as such it could not be used in the temple treasury. So they bought a potter's field with it as a burial ground for foreigners—the very field in which Judas had so miserably hanged himself. It was afterwards known as the Field of Blood (Matthew 27:3–10 and Acts 1:18–19).

The legends that followed the other apostles in the apocryphal writings could not, of course, follow Judas beyond the Field of Blood, but that did not hinder them from inventing bizarre stories of his early life possessed by the devil and attacking the infant Christ. The Gnostic *Gospel of Judas* even turns him into something of a hero, suggesting that Judas alone understood the truth that mankind would be redeemed by the death of Jesus. However, generally even these false writings, and certainly all the early church leaders, portrayed Judas as a terrible warning of deceit and betrayal. His name has continued in folk-lore, idioms and legends, and as late as the seventeenth century a priest from Vienna wrote a story, in its English title, *The Arch Knave, or The History of Judas from the cradle to the gallows*.

The remorse of Judas was not repentance. The word used in Matthew 27:3 and translated by the phrase 'seized with remorse', is something less than true repentance and implies nothing more than a sorrowful regret. Like Esau centuries earlier, Judas 'found no place for repentance' (Hebrews 12:17 NKJV). He was 'doomed to destruction' (John 17:12), and finally went 'where he belongs' (Acts 1:25). In the words of Jesus himself: 'It would be better for him if he had not been born' (Matthew 26:24). But is Judas so very different from millions who, having heard the message of the kingdom and, having read the story of his perfect life, then reject all that they know? Or is he so different from those who once accepted the story as true, and made a profession of loyalty to Christ and then betray him by joining the world in its indifference or opposition to the Saviour? It would surely be better if these had not been born either.

However, as if it was not possible for the account of the apostles to close on such a bitter note, God had planned for a replacement of the betrayer by one who was worthy to 'take his place of leadership.'

Matthias—the forgotten apostle

'Then they cast lots, and the lot fell to Matthias; so he was added to the eleven apostles' Acts 1:26

We know nothing about his home, family, occupation or future activity, and for most Christians, even if they have taken the trouble to learn the names of the twelve apostles, they have probably overlooked this one. He must be one of God's little people because few seem to know about him! His name means 'gift of Yahweh', so he clearly came from good Jewish stock, and perhaps he was named after one of the great heroes of Israel's fight for freedom, Mattathias Maccabeus the father of the five Maccabean sons who, some two hundred years earlier, had fought for independence against the Syrians.

We are not introduced to Matthias by name in the Gospel records at all, though that is where the main part of his story belongs. Acts 1 concerns the days following the resurrection and ascension of Christ, and the disciples were meeting in the upper room in a home in Jerusalem; it was very likely that this was the home of Mary the mother of John Mark, because that is where the believers were meeting in Acts 12, and when Peter had been shut up in prison by Herod and then let out by the angel, he knew exactly where to go to find the rest (v 12). Back in Acts 1 the disciples were 'constantly' in prayer (v 14), and there were a good number of them. We are told that the eleven apostles were present, plus the women who had been assisting and providing for Jesus and the apostles, plus the mother of Jesus and his brothers. According to v 15 there were one hundred and twenty in all, though elsewhere in the city there must have been many more followers of the new Way, since Paul could record at least five hundred who had seen Jesus after his resurrection (1 Corinthians 15:6).

The necessity of Matthias' election

Peter raised an issue that at the time may hardly have seemed relevant. These were dangerous days for the followers of 'the Way', and the fear of the Jews and Romans was still with them. Besides, ringing in their ears was the recent challenge to world-wide evangelism and the promise of the Holy Spirit. In the light of the great challenges and possibilities that lay ahead, did it really matter that they should maintain the number of apostles at the exact figure of twelve? Would it not be much more sensible to focus on the one hundred and twenty, or the five hundred?

However, Peter had a more significant and overriding reason for his claim that, 'it is necessary to choose one of the men who have been with us the whole time the Lord Jesus went in and out among us' (vs 21). The appointment of Matthias was not emotional, as if Peter was saying: 'Let's keep the number to twelve because that is what Jesus would have wanted.' Nor was it merely practical: 'We need twelve and not eleven if we are ever to accomplish our task.' After all, they did not replace the apostle James when, not long afterwards, he was executed on Herod's orders (Acts 12:2). Peter's reasoning was biblical: 'The Scripture had to be fulfilled' in the betrayal and death of Judas (Acts 1:16), and equally it must be fulfilled in the appointment of his successor.

Peter had learned from his Master that all things associated with the life of Christ were 'according to the Scriptures.' He could recall that some time before, when Jesus was debating with the chief priests and the elders in Jerusalem, he had said to them: 'Have you never read in the Scriptures: "The stone the builders rejected has become the capstone"' (Matthew 21:42).

More recently in Gethsemane, the Lord reminded those who came to arrest him that, if he wished, he could call on twelve legions of angels: 'But how then would the Scriptures be fulfilled that say it must happen in this way?' (Matthew 26:53). Then, the breathless report of the two disciples who lived in Emmaus confirmed the study of the Scriptures that the risen Christ had shared with them: 'And beginning with Moses and all the Prophets, he explained to them what was said in all the Scriptures concerning himself' (Luke 24:27). Shortly afterwards, among the apostles, 'He opened their minds so they could understand the Scriptures. He told them, 'This is what is written: The Christ will suffer and rise from the dead on the third day' (Luke 24:45–46).

So far, all the Scriptures that referred to Christ had been fulfilled, but from that Bible study in the upper room, Peter could see one particular omission. Now, for the first time, Peter himself was quoting from the Old Testament. First, he referred to Psalm 69:25, 'May their place be deserted; let there be no-one to dwell in their tents'; though Peter changed the plural of David's enemies into the singular to refer to Judas. This was followed by Psalm 109:8 'May his days be few; may another take his place of leadership.' Why did Peter go to these two psalms, since they were not thought of as 'messianic' by the Jews? Peter was quite clear that although David wrote these two Psalms, it was the Holy Spirit who spoke 'though the mouth of David concerning Judas' (v 16).

There was, of course, another specific reference in the Old Testament that Peter was familiar with: 'Even my close friend, whom I trusted, he who shared my bread, has lifted up his heel against me' (Psalm 41:9). Peter knew that this verse referred to Judas, because Jesus had quoted it when warning of the betrayal (John 13:18). It is likely that in the detailed Bible study that our Lord gave to his disciples, recorded in Luke 24:27, these two psalms were included. Both psalms are what we call 'imprecatory psalms' in which David calls down the judgment of God upon those who so bitterly opposed him. But he did not do this in a spirit of cruel personal vindictiveness, but as a prophetic denunciation; it was the Holy Spirit speaking 'through the mouth of David' (Acts 1:16).

What was true of all the enemies of God, was true especially of Judas, who committed perhaps the most heinous sin in history. In the early centuries of the church, Psalm 109 was known as the 'Iscariotic psalm'—the psalm of Iscariot—and it was certainly appropriate as a psalm of a traitor: So much of it could refer to Judas: 'In return for my friendship they accuse me' (v 4). Peter was not suggesting that David was aware that his psalm had a prophetic dimension to it, but that the Holy Spirit, who moved David in his writing, certainly had that in mind. David, on his part, wrote of his own enemies, just as he had written of his own experiences in Psalm 22, though clearly, unknown to him, there was a definite Messianic application.

Peter's use of two seemingly obscure verses from the Psalms reveals just how steeped he was in his Old Testament Scriptures. He also knew that once you understand the Scriptures, you are under an obligation to be obedient to them. This is why he concluded: 'Therefore it is necessary to choose one of the men who have been with us the whole time...' (Acts 1:21).

The qualification for Matthias' election

For anyone to take the place of an apostle, he had to be a man who had been a disciple for the 'whole time' from the baptism by John the Baptist to the ascension of Jesus Christ (Acts 1:21–22). This was important for a number of reasons.

In the first place it would reveal the candidate's biblical discernment and consistency. From his understanding of the Scriptures, Matthias had obviously been expecting the Messiah to come and thus accepted the message of John the Baptist and submitted to his baptism. As soon as John the Baptist began to point out that Jesus of Nazareth was the Messiah, Matthias had turned his allegiance to the Christ. More than this, he had stayed with the disciples throughout the long haul and with the approaching dark clouds of betrayal and trial. Many came and went. Others wanted to join, but when they considered the cost, it was too great and they backed off. Nor was Matthias a recent convert who had only joined in once the news of the resurrection was broadcast. Here was a man who could stay the course. Matthias is never mentioned once in the Gospels, but he was there all the time. Unknowingly, he was waiting on the substitute bench.

Matthias was almost certainly one of the seventy who were sent out by Jesus to preach the gospel of the kingdom; at least Eusebius, the third century church historian, is sure of this. There is a slight variation among the available Greek texts for Luke 10:1, some read 'seventy-two' and others read 'seventy'. Seventy seems the better reading, not only because it follows the majority and the better texts, but also that figure matches the seventy elders elected by Moses on the advice of Jethro his father in law (Exodus 18:17–27 and Numbers 11:16–25). But whatever the number, Matthias had gone out with a clear message, clear authority, and had seen God at work (Luke 10:17).

Matthias was also a personal witness to the resurrection of Christ. This was of fundamental importance as Peter made clear in 2 Peter 1:16, 'We did not follow cleverly invented stories when we told you about the power and coming of our Lord Jesus Christ, but we were eye-witnesses of his majesty.' Since most of the apostles were to give their lives for the sake of the kingdom, it was essential that they had no doubts about a core doctrine of their message. If there is no resurrection then, as Paul so plainly declared in 1 Corinthians 15, there is no gospel, no forgiveness and no hope.

But a further qualification for his election was the clear humility of Matthias. Matthias was not chosen to be one of the initial twelve, but there had been no jockeying for position; he clearly was not 'put out' simply because he was not among the first names on the A-team. Had he been of the same mind as Diotrephes 'who loves to be first' (3 John 9) there is no doubt at all that his name would never have come into the discussion, let alone been entered on the slate of the finalists. Matthias showed a humble acceptance that whatever his task, it was a privilege to serve the King of kings. All this is vital for any Christian leader: biblical discernment, consistent service, a total commitment to the resurrection, and a man of humility. He clearly had a good reputation among the other apostles and the believers more generally. He had already served and served well.

The reputation of those who are chosen for Christian leadership is vital. Of the deacons in Acts 6:3 the apostles looked for 'men from among you who are known to be full of the Spirit and wisdom'. That phrase 'men from among you' is as important as 'full of the Spirit and wisdom'. In the same way Acts 16:2 notes of Timothy that 'The brothers at Lystra and Iconium spoke well of him.' Paul looked for 'the men you approve' to take the offering up to Jerusalem (1 Corinthians 16:3). And he instructed Timothy that leaders 'Must be above reproach ... He must also have a good reputation with outsiders' (1 Timothy 3:2,7). Paul constantly commended his workers, and specified why. For example, to the church at Colossae and to Philemon, Epaphras is described as a dear fellow-servant, a faithful prisoner, a faithful minister of Christ, wrestling in prayer, and working hard. Let any man considered for leadership in the church be tested by his peers and the world outside.

The method of Matthias' election

Two men were put forward by all the believers present. Why two? Clearly both Joseph and Matthias were equal nominees for the position and the apostles simply could not decide. Whether they were divided on the matter, or all equally unsure, will have to remain uncertain for us. They had done all they could and whittled the names down to two. The appointment, therefore, was partly the result of human debate and discussion: they met and talked and reasoned and evaluated. They did not resort to the lot among the entire number of qualified believers present, they discussed and agreed on two possible names. To resolve the issue, they resorted to prayer—unsurprisingly, and then they cast lots—also unsurprisingly.

The use of a lot was more common in the first century and earlier than now for deciding significant issues. Magistrates in Athens were elected by this method, and whilst the sailors in charge of Jonah's ship (Jonah 1:7) are not a model for us, it was commonplace for the lot to be used for serious issues under the old covenant of Israel. The division of the land among the twelve tribes of Israel was determined by lot (Numbers 34:13), as was the goat to be slaughtered and the one to be released on the Day of Atonement (Leviticus 16:8). Similarly, the roster of service in the tabernacle among the sons of Aaron was decided by lot: 'They divided them impartially by drawing lots' (1 Chronicles 24:5 see also 25:8). Its common use is evidenced by the conviction in Proverbs 16:33 that, 'The lot is cast into the lap, but its every decision is from the LORD.'

It was not a dice that was used, but slates with the names written on them; the slates would be shaken in a container, and the one that fell out first was chosen. There is no reference to Christians resorting to this method from here on, neither in Acts nor among the wealth of instructions to the young churches in the letters of Paul, Peter, James, John or Jude. This episode forms a bridge, midway between the congregation in the Old Testament, and that in the New. Under the old regime, there was no consulting of the people generally, the 'lot' was the first and the last resort.

It was a new experience for any of these apostles, and the others, to be expected to play a part in the selection process. Jesus had not consulted any of the disciples before he chose the first twelve; in fact, he withdrew to be alone with his Father (Luke 6:12–13). He had many disciples before the apostles were appointed (Mark 3:7, 13–14) and clearly used that period to prepare them for the special service of the Twelve. For three years the Master craftsman had shown this disparate band how he could make the most unlikely group gel as a team. Had he left the decisions for an election by their peers, it would be unimaginable for Peter to have voted for Simon the Zealot, or for Simon the Zealot to have voted for Matthew the tax collector. But now, three years later, they had at least learnt what to look for, and to believe in the power of Christ to change lives.

In its infancy, the church consulted *and* used the lot. But from here on the method of choosing leaders would be prayer and reliance on the wisdom given by the Holy Spirit as they discussed the issues among themselves. This was the very first decision the apostles, and therefore the church, had to make on their own and without the visible presence of Christ. This is the only reason (and the only occasion) why the Lord of the church conceded to their use of the lot. From now on they would have to grow up into mature judgement. Only a childishly immature church would resort to such a method of decision-making in the future.

For the choice of the first 'deacons', the apostles gathered all the disciples together—whether the seventy or the one hundred and twenty or more—and handed the decision over to them: 'Brothers, choose seven men from among you ...' (Acts 6:3); this proposal 'pleased the whole group' (v 5). Later the ground rules for choosing leaders were laid out especially in the letters of Paul to Timothy and Titus. That is our pattern today.

The assurance of Matthias' election

Matthias had the privilege of knowing that his election was in fulfilment of a biblical promise. He was the only disciple of Christ whose future election as an apostle had been specifically underwritten in Old Testament prophecy. Matthias was aware that when the Holy Spirit moved David to pen those two passages in the Psalms, he did so with Matthias in mind. When that fact dawned on this substitute apostle, it must have humbled him even more. His particular role, if not his very name, had been recorded in Scripture nine hundred years earlier.

But this was not the only unique fact about the choice of Matthias. He was short-listed by all the believers, and this means that he was the first

Christian worker or leader to have been chosen by his peers. It would have been a constant encouragement to Matthias to recall that he had joined the apostles with the full support and approval of such a large number of disciples; and that was a pattern set for the church in the future. In addition to this, the election of Matthias was confirmed by the casting of a lot. This, as we noted, was an intermediate stage in the growing maturity of the church. It would be evidence that he was the one 'you have chosen' (Acts 1:24). Significantly, the same verb is used in v 2 when Luke referred to the apostles whom Jesus 'had chosen'. At this time, such confirmation was valuable because the infant church needed reassurance, but in future it would not be like this.

However, the phrase 'who you have chosen' was much more than a reminder of the immediate result of the way the lot fell out, it was an encouragement to believe that for all the servants of Christ, who are chosen 'before the foundation of the world' (Ephesians 1:4; see also Revelation 13:8), their precise ministry and service is also chosen. When the word of the Lord came to Jeremiah saying, 'Before I formed you in the womb I knew you, before you were born I set you apart; I appointed you as a prophet to the nations' (Jeremiah 1:5), that was no more true of Jeremiah than of any whom Christ calls to be his disciples. Paul also knew that God had 'set me apart from birth and called me by his grace' (Galatians 1:15), but so does every Christian. Matthias could constantly bask in the reassurance of that. God has big plans, eternal plans, for the lives of all his little people.

The challenge of Matthias' election

The role that Matthias was to take on, was a 'place of leadership'. If he was already one of the seventy who had been sent out to preach the kingdom of God and to see miracles happen, then he was not unused to a position of leadership. But this was something very different. For the first time in the story of the church, the word for 'leadership' used in verse 20 is the word *episcopos* in the Greek—one of two words that in the rest of the New Testament describe the role of a leader in the church. The two words are *presbuteros*, generally translated as 'elder', and *episcopos* which is the 'overseer' of 1 Timothy 3:1–2; Titus 1:7 and 1 Peter 2:25. In the Hebrew of

Psalm 109:8, the Hebrew word *pecudah* carries the same meaning of one who watches over others and has responsibility for them. Here is another unique fact about the appointment of Matthias: although all the apostles were called to serve in this capacity, Matthias was the first to be granted that specific title. Once again, the structure of the church was being carefully put in place without the gathered disciples probably being aware of how significant all this was.

Perhaps even more important is the phrase: 'He was added to the eleven apostles' (v 26). That may sound obvious, but it was very significant for Matthias. It must have been awesome for Matthias to remember whose place he was taking! The apparent loyalty and successful activity of Judas was nothing more than a cover for his subversive actions, grasping greed and cruel betrayal. Christ had known this all along, but none of the disciples had guessed it. This was a serious warning to all who come close to the work of the Spirit and yet fall away. Matthias could not be unaware of the meaning, even though the words had not yet been penned, of a later specific warning: 'It is impossible for those who have once been enlightened, who have tasted the heavenly gift, who have shared in the Holy Spirit, who have tasted the goodness of the word of God and the powers of the coming age, if they fall away, to be brought back to repentance, because to their loss they are crucifying the Son of God all over again and subjecting him to public disgrace' (Hebrews 6:4–6). All that was tragically only too true of Judas Iscariot.

With Judas in mind, Matthias would never forget that just because he had been chosen to make up the number of the apostles, that was no excuse for a slack approach to his life of responsible leadership. To be chosen for leadership would be no guarantee of faithful continuance. Indeed, the title of 'apostle' was not an authorization into heaven. This solemn fact must always balance the 'you have chosen' phrase. We may rest in the knowledge of the final security of those who are chosen by God, to such an extent that we forget the doctrine of final perseverance. The New Testament is full of warnings that those who profess Christ should examine themselves, make sure of their salvation, and see to it that none has a sinful and unbelieving heart that turns away from the living God. Office and titles in the church, from the very highest to the lowest, are no guarantee of salvation, any more than are the praise and good reputation from men. Judas Iscariot towers as a serious warning to all God's little people.

The fact that Matthias was following in the place of Judas would inevitably remind him of the responsibility of leadership. James warned, 'Not many of you should presume to be teachers, my brothers, because you know that we who teach will be judged more strictly' (James 3:1). There is no doubt about that. Exactly what the judgement will be for those who presume to lead, and yet lead astray, I do not know, but to be added to the list of apostles was clearly not a passport into glory.

If it is true that the apostle John was alone among the twelve in dying peacefully of old age, Matthias had yet to learn what suffering lay before him. Tradition offers to come to our aid of course, though we can lay little trust in its contradictory claims. Some say that Matthias preached in Jerusalem where he was stoned to death, and others in Ethiopia where he was crucified. Some of the early church leaders, like Origen, Eusebius and others, refer to a *Gospel of Matthias*, though they wisely call it a false writing and attribute it to a heretic and not to our Matthias. This is unsurprising since almost all the apostles have some false writing credited to them. The devil has had little better to do over the past two thousand years than to ape the works of God.

If we have never realised it before, we should now see that Matthias, another of God's little people—and another whose words and actions are not recorded for us—enters at a crucial point in the formation of the church, and his qualification, election and the challenge set before him, still carries a message for the church today. His name means 'God's gift', and he certainly was.

Index

Index